CONTEMPORARY GANG ISSUES:

AN INSIDE VIEW

by

Sandra S. Stone, Ph.D.
Editor

CONTEMPORARY GANG ISSUES: AN INSIDE VIEW

by

Sandra S. Stone, Ph.D.
Editor

ISBN 0-9665155-6-0

Library of Congress Catalog Card Number: 00-1333627

OCLC# 45010683

New Chicago School Press, Inc
P.O. Box 929
Peotone. IL 60468-0929

This book is dedicated to my husband, Tony, who gave up time
with me during evenings and weekends so I could work on it,
and to our children, Bailey and Adam,
who keep me ever mindful of why we all need
to be committed to ending gang violence.
I love them dearly; they are my inspiration.

EDITOR'S PREFACE

The papers included in this monograph are based on a study sponsored by the National Gang Crime Research Center. The authors and editor would like to thank Dr. George W. Knox, NGCRC Director, for allowing us the opportunity to participate in this important work. We would also like to thank the NGCRC for publication of this monograph so that we can share what we have learned with others interested in the study of gangs.

TABLE OF CONTENTS

CHAPTER ONE

INTRODUCTION AND SUMMARY OF PROJECT GANGFACT

Sandra S. Stone, Ph.D.
State University of West Georgia

Social scientists have studied and written about gangs for decades, yet interest in the topic remains robust. One reason may be that even as we study them, gang members, gang dynamics and gangs themselves change – sometimes dramatically, sometimes in more subtle ways. Certainly no one would argue that the gangs portrayed in the media in the 1950s (i.e. West Side Story) are very different from the gangs portrayed in the media more recently (i.e. Colors; Boyz N the Hood; Blood In, Blood Out; American History X). Regardless of their structure and activities, however, gangs have in the past and continue in the present to exert a significant influence on the culture. One only has to look around, especially in more urban environments, to witness the influence of gangs, particularly on young people. Gang life is glorified in rap lyrics; gang attire is replicated by youths from adolescents to very young children; gang symbols and language are written, gesticulated and spoken in public places; and gang values, attitudes and behaviors are imitated, and sometimes assimilated, by an increasing number of young people in all segments of society. In addition, gangs continue to pose increasing and ever-changing challenges for all segments of the criminal justice system -- law enforcement, courts and corrections. Thus, in an attempt to understand these phenomena, we must likewise attempt to keep our knowledge of gangs and gang activities current.

Many books and articles have been published on gangs, especially in the past decade or so, but most of these have focused on particular groups, particular locations, particular gang or gang-related activities, or particular issues of concern to schools, police, communities, courts, or other segments of society. Little work has been done to examine gang issues from a national perspective, gathering information on gang life directly from gang members themselves. The information that will be presented in this book will address that deficit.

In 1995, the National Gang Crime Research Center, located in Chicago, embarked upon a major study of gangs and various aspects of gang life. The study was referred to as Project GANGFACT (Gang Field Assessment of Crime Threat). The National Gang Crime Research Center (NGCRC) was founded in 1990 and its track record of research productivity is considerable. The Center also publishes a professional quarterly journal, the *Journal of Gang Research*, and Center staff provide assessment, research, and training services about gangs and security threat/risk groups across the country. The mission of the Center is to promote and carry out research to more effectively educate the public about how to reduce the crime and violence from gangs and gang members.

Project GANGFACT was conducted through a collaborative effort with 28 researchers in 17 different states. All the researchers have a positive track record of scholarship and service in their respective agencies and volunteered to participate in this study. This study was not funded through any external sources. No one received any supplemental pay, and, in fact, many of us personally covered the costs of the study at our respective sites. This "task force" approach developed by the National Gang Crime Research Center has a history of previous successes, including other large-scale research projects carried out in recent years such as: Project GANGPINT, Project GANGECON, and Project GANGGUNS. In the task force approached developed by the NGCRC, each member of the consortium takes individual responsibility for a significant data collection contribution towards the national sampling goal. This is done in their local areas or in geographical areas not reached by other members of the consortium. The data reduction tasks are handled by the NGCRC. It is the duty of the consortium members to develop strong positive ties to local correctional authorities for the purpose of research access. Follow-up after data collection is essential to maintaining ongoing positive relationships with host sites. Host sites are those criminal justice agencies (jails, prisons, juvenile detention centers, boot camps, long-term juvenile correctional institutions, and private residential correctional facilities) who allow a Project GANGFACT researcher to collect local data. A host site, in return, receives a major service free of charge: a customized local research report based on an analysis of data collected from that site. The report is confidential and provided to the site administrator. Project GANGFACT provides this local, rapid, useful feedback at no expense and as a public service to the host agency. A host site can remain completely anonymous if the administrator so chooses, meaning that site will not be identified in a traceable way in the acknowledgements section of the final report.

The researchers who participated are from a diverse and interdisciplinary spectrum (criminology, health care, special education, criminal justice practitioners, etc) and utilized a somewhat different approach than what is usually found in the literature. Some projects survey police chiefs or social workers, and ask their opinions on the scope and extent of the gang problem. Other projects analyze police records to see what can be learned from arrest reports about gang activity. Still others study the community's attitude toward gangs, gang members, and gang victimization. In contrast, Project GANGFACT used the individual gang member as the unit of analysis. The research strategy is the classic "self-report" methodology in survey research, enhanced with additional attention to validity and reliability issues. The idea was to collect new primary data directly from gang members. In an effort to maximize the number of gang members responding to the survey, Project GANGFACT targeted the confined, predominantly juvenile, offender population in 17 states. Although the survey was anonymous, with no identifying information on respondents recorded, the research project still had to be approved by a number of Institutional Review boards in the states affected. In some states legal opinions had to be obtained that would exempt the researchers from parental notification policies. In California, a detailed court motion had to be filed along these same lines in order to obtain approval for access to incarcerated juveniles. Access to incarcerated adults proved a somewhat easier task. We found that the anonymous survey process works most effectively in these settings if the respondents are "rewarded" for their assistance. Most sites used in Project GANGFACT, therefore, made use of such rewards. These rewards varied from providing a $1.00 donation to the inmate's account in an Iowa jail, to providing bags of chips or candy bars to respondents inside juvenile detention centers.

A 100-item survey questionnaire was administered to approximately 10,000 juvenile and adult inmates in 75 different correctional facilities. The study includes 4,140 self-reported gang members. To our knowledge, the study is the largest and most comprehensive of its kind ever completed. Thus, we have a unique database to work from, which includes information about the personal lives of the individuals surveyed, detailed information about gang structure and activities from those who reported having ever been a member of a gang, and first-hand accounts of their continued gang activity while in correctional facilities. The purpose for the book, then, is to share the findings from this study, highlighting those issues we believe provide some new information, insight and/or understanding regarding factors associated with gang involvement, gang structure and activities, and the impact of gangs on the criminal justice system. Each participating researcher was allowed to contribute questions that pertained to their particular area(s) of interest. The issues we were most concerned about were why some children get involved in gangs and others do not, whether the gangs are really organized and highly structured or loosely formed groups of kids that more or less "hang out" together, and the impact of gangs on the criminal justice system, especially corrections. The analyses of our particular questions were further developed by some researchers into the papers that comprise this book.

The book is divided into four main sections, with a total of nine chapters, some of which include recommendations for interventions. In addition to this introduction, the first section also contains a more detailed discussion of the methodology utilized in collecting data for the study. The author of the introduction, I have been interested in and actively studying gangs since the late 1980s. I have worked with the Atlanta Police Department and the GA Department of Juvenile Justice on gang issues, and I now teach a course on gangs at the State University of West Georgia, where I am employed. Dr. George Knox, founder and Director of the National Gang Crime Research Center, wrote the methodology chapter. He has been involved in gang research for many years, working closely with a variety of criminal justice agencies, schools and community organizations. Dr. Knox has written extensively on the subject of gangs, including a major, comprehensive textbook.

The second section of the book, which contains the most material, will cover different issues associated with gang involvement. The first chapter in that section, Chapter Three, is on bullying. Research, our own and others', shows that either being a bully or being a victim of a bully increases the likelihood that a child will become involved in a gang. They may do so to get support for their bullying behavior and/or to get protection from the bullying behavior of others. The author of this chapter, Dr. Shirley Holmes, has been a leading researcher in this field for several years. In addition to teaching in the Education Department at North Georgia College and State University, she works closely with several school systems to address this problem. Chapter Four in that section will discuss different family dynamics of gang vs. non-gang members. Dr. Jodet-Marie Harris, who wrote that chapter, teaches in the Education Department at Jackson State University (MS) and works with families of gang members. Following, in Chapter Five, is a discussion of risk factors for joining a gang, which I wrote. This chapter relates the findings from the study on motivations to join a gang and characteristics found to be significantly associated with those motivations. Risk factors at the individual, family, school and community levels are identified. The final chapter in this section, Chapter Six, looks at the gang involvement of girls. An increasing number of girls are getting involved in mainstream gang activities, and no one is entirely sure why. Information is also lacking on the nature and extent of their involvement. Chapter Six will explore those issues. Ms. Kathleen Aquino, the author of that chapter, is a health educator with the Los Angeles County Health Department and has a great deal of experience working with adolescents, including adolescents in juvenile detention centers.

The third section, which only has one chapter, Chapter Seven, will address the level of organization of gangs, based on the findings from the study. That chapter was written by Dr. Alice Franklin Elder, Director of Research at the Ohio Department of Youth Services. She has been actively studying and writing about the gang situation in that state for several years.

The fourth, and last, section will explore some of the issues that corrections officials in both the juvenile and adult systems have to deal with when gang members are incarcerated. What we have learned is that juveniles, like adults, often continue engaging in gang-related activities while in correctional facilities and programs. This poses an increased threat not only to other inmates, but to staff in those facilities/programs as well. Dr. Elder and I wrote the chapter on gang activities inside correctional facilities, Chapter Eight, based on findings from the study and our own experiences working in the juvenile correctional systems in Ohio and Georgia. The last chapter, Chapter Nine, written by Dr. Knox, suggests a classification system corrections officials can use to identify gang members that are likely to pose a threat to security. Once identified, these individuals can be dealt with in a way that decreases their risks to invoke harm. This system was validated using data from the study.

It is our belief that only when we better understand the appeal of gang life for young people and the needs that get met for them in the gang that do not get met in other areas of their lives can we intervene more effectively. We also need to better understand the nature and extent of the structure and organization of gangs today in order to formulate more effective interventions at a systemic level. And further, we need to develop tools for criminal justice officials, particularly those working in correctional settings, to identify gang members, assess risks, and develop management techniques to enhance the safety of staff and other inmates in confined settings.

Gangs have been a part of American culture since at least Colonial times, when groups of highwaymen would rob unsuspecting travelers, and there is no indication that gangs will disappear anytime soon. Consequently, it is in our best interest to understand as much as we can about the appeal of gangs to young people, how gangs function, the conditions under which gangs thrive, and effective prevention/intervention strategies. It is our hope that the information shared in this book will add to the reader's knowledge and understanding of this very complex social phenomenon, and that as a result, he or she will be better prepared to provide alternatives to the young people in his or her personal life and/or larger community.

CHAPTER TWO

METHODOLOGY OF PROJECT GANGFACT

George W. Knox, Ph.D.
National Gang Crime Research Center

INTRODUCTION

The purpose of this section is to explain the research methodology for Project GANGFACT. The section outlines the research process from beginning to end. Special attention is paid to issues of validity and reliability.

ITEM DEVELOPMENT AND PRETESTING THE SURVEY INSTRUMENT

All members of the Project GANGFACT research task force at an early stage in the research process developed specific hypotheses they would explore and test. This meant that every researcher developed and submitted specific questions or items to be included in the survey instrument. These questions in the preliminary item pool were then distributed for review, critiqued, revised and then finally tested in a pretest of the finalized survey instrument. With $N = 28$ different researchers in this national gang research consortium, obviously there were many different types of hypotheses that would be explored in the research, even though the primary theme examined aspects of gang prevention and gang intervention generally.

The pre-testing of the instrument was conducted in a high gang density juvenile correctional institution in the mid-west. This is a famous site for the Chicago-school of criminological research. The site staff was very skeptical that the youths could, in fact, complete the survey, but most were able to complete it in a very short period of time. In fact, this facility, containing nearly 500 youths in short term detention, was completely surveyed in a very short period of time; the researchers were able to get in and out of the facility within a two-hour period. Several members of the research task force were present for this pre-testing; they made observations and debriefed some of the respondents (i.e., asking them to report questions they did not understand, words they did not understand, phrases they did not understand, etc.) and some of the staff. Through this process the survey instrument was further modified to make necessary changes identified from the pre-testing. Actually, very few changes had to be made. The pre-test sample was known in advance to contain gang members. We expected that there would be some respondents who would not know about some of the detailed issues of gang life; any non-gang member would not be privy to the socialization and training afforded by a gang (i.e., learning its language or sub-cultural argot, its rules, its code, etc).

After the survey instrument was field tested, we felt comfortable, as described in the section on validity below, that the instrument was capable of measuring what it sought to measure.

SAMPLING OVER 4,000 GANG MEMBERS

The type of research that samples only from one city or one state has historically been a source of confounding and confusing research results in the gang research arena. We felt we needed to capture gang members where they can really be found -- on the street, and in custody. Our research strategy was one that, therefore, focused on a variety of social contexts in order to obtain a sample of 5,000 gang members. Mostly, we sought to have representative national data, and therefore, we focused our research strategy on multiple states, in large and small jurisdictions. We did not reach our original goal of N = 5,000 gang members, but we came respectably close in generating a gang member sample of over 4,000.

Figure 1, which can be found at the end of the chapter, shows the type of social context by the sample size of gang members from these sites in twenty states. Over 75 different sites in 17 states were used for data collection in the research reported here. In all contexts, a saturation sampling technique was sought. This meant everyone in the social context was asked to participate in the research. Sometimes incentives were used, and this meant upwards of 90 percent of the populations in these contexts cooperating. Our sample of gang members, therefore, includes juveniles and adults in custody.

INTERNAL CONTROLS ON DATA QUALITY

A number of precautions and safeguards were undertaken during the survey process to ensure the highest possible quality in the data collected.

Covert Observation. During the actual collection of data at some sites, there was the opportunity for covert observation. This involved several of the jail or juvenile correctional sites where it was possible to watch the inmates completing the questionnaires on closed circuit television or through observation areas. Thus, in some jail sites it was possible for the researchers to hand out pencils and surveys and then in a control room watch the inmate behavior in their cell areas on the security video monitors. In no case did we see collaboration or any systematic tampering (i.e., one inmate filling out more than one questionnaire). There was no evidence of any collective fraud on the part of inmates in completing the questionnaires. As in other settings, this was presented as a "very personal" survey. Almost all inmates and others surveyed in other sites were remarkably cooperative. In most sites, for example, there was always at least one researcher present at all times inside each classroom while the questionnaires were being filled out.

Overt Observation. Overt observation was the rule of thumb in all sites, as one or more of the principal researchers were on hand at all sites to watch and observe the process of data collection. This also afforded the opportunity of introducing another methodological safeguard to evaluate the quality of our data collection. For example, gender is a specific forced-choice item on the questionnaire, but it was also a variable coded during overt observation immediately after collecting the questionnaires. In all the jails, in the west-coast sites, and in Chicago sites, we took an additional overt observation precaution during the data collection process. This entailed physically marking the physical source documents with a code for gender. Thus, all male and female respondents could then be assessed in terms of attempts at deception with regard to gender. This code assigned by the researchers as an observation taken during a close social contact (i.e., collecting the survey instruments one at a time) was then compared with the respondents' forced-choice response. A random response pattern or a fraudulent response pattern could possibly be evident in a case where the overt observation of gender did not match the self-reported gender in response to the survey question. Lying about gender was seen in only a couple of cases, and where it was detected, the entire survey instrument was not used. Thus, a few cases were eliminated for obvious attempts at deception.

Zero Tolerance for Data Entry or Transcription Errors. All survey data stored electronically for purposes of computerized statistical analysis were cross-checked against source documents (i.e., the survey instruments). The data were checked and re-checked and contain no validity threat from transcription errors in the data reduction process. Most of the data entry was performed by one of the Ph.D. researchers or a Ph.D. candidate statistical typist. Some of the data were keyed to disk by highly trained advanced students serving as interns to the National Gang Crime Research Center, and their work was thoroughly checked.

Few Unusable Survey Instruments Detected. In most of the sites and social contexts used for data collection, a saturation sampling method was used: everyone in the site was asked to complete the questionnaire. Small honorariums were used in some of the sites, and in these sites we could casually check the surveys to ensure they were fully completed before giving out the honorariums. In very few instances were unusable questionnaires returned. Far less than one percent of the surveys was incomplete, and those typically involved someone who would check every response to every question, or expressed some similar form of non-cooperation. Participation in the research was a voluntary action, and for the most part, a very large majority of the persons at all sites participated and provided high cooperation. The most hostile reaction the gang members had to the survey was to the question about their life expectancy: at what age they expected they would die. However, we got the distinct impression that most respondents, including those in custody, were highly motivated to complete the questionnaires, in one sense because this provided an interesting distraction from the boredom of routine regular activities. In only rare instances, then, did we obtain "tainted" survey instruments: those what were obviously fraudulently completed or not capable of being interpreted, where the respondent was, for the most part, non-cooperative. Thus, no tainted data are included in our analysis because in the very few cases where the respondent was less than cooperative, their survey instruments were discarded.

An Acceptable Level of Trust Was Established. While our approach was essentially the same with everyone regardless of the social context, in the jail and secure contexts extra efforts were made to provide an adequate introduction and explanation to the respondents. At least one or more of the researchers were typically on hand in the correctional environments studied, where they approached each cell-house area or living area and explained in detail the purpose of the survey research. In the correctional settings, it was not uncommon for joking comments to be heard from the respondents about criminal justice officials, or critical comments towards the criminal justice system generally. Friendly dialogue was common in all social contexts, because the researchers often took time after the survey to answer verbal inquiries and listen to concerns and issues of the respondents. While the survey asks for no name, and its printed title is "THE 1996 ANONYMOUS NATIONAL YOUTH SURVEY," and while we explained verbally that we did not want their names because this was a very personal type of questionnaire, it was not uncommon in some instances for respondents to still write in their names and provide other unsolicited information. Several offered to become paid informants, or desired personal interviews such as this respondent from a mid-western site: "I can tell you a lot more about the _____ gang; please ask Officer Smith if you can talk to me in private." Such messages of "snitches" willing to sell their souls were common in all sites across the nation.

In nearly all research sites or settings, one or more of the co-principal investigators was always present, along with one or more research assistants who were always on hand in each room or area. Further, to ensure the privacy of the responses, the respondents were told that their teacher or program supervisor would never actually see or touch the surveys. Thus, we collected all surveys directly from the respondents in and out of the correctional settings. A large number of students and volunteers assisted Project GANGFACT in 17 different states. Based on the above procedures, our respect for the respondents regarding the privacy of their responses, <u>and</u> our observations of the process of data collection, we feel that a sufficient level of trust was established with respondents to get relatively honest answers.

We have only one caveat that all criminological researchers should be recognizing themselves: offenders have the tendency to over-report their positive attributes and under-report those attributes which might have a stigma attached, and the kind of gang members we are studying are more often than not offenders. Regardless of social context, this tendency operates in all areas of research on real offenders, and gang offenders are no different. We also recognize, and this tendency works to our methodological advantage, that offenders are more likely to honestly report the deviance of their friends and associates than their own deviance. Thus, many of the questions or focal areas of our research ask them about "others", i.e., members of their gang.

<u>High Cognition on the Meaning of the Survey Items Implies Clearly We Are Measuring What We Purport To Measure</u>. A large number of respondents across social contexts, but particularly those in custody, had the tendency to write notes and memoranda style comments in the margins of the survey instrument on a variety of issues. These are highly emotive comments implying clear cognition of the true meaning of the survey items or questions. Several examples of this kind of "running" commentary and shared written communication from respondents illustrate our assumption that respondents clearly understood the meaning of the questions. Not one survey respondent returned the survey instrument and claimed not to understand the questions. Not one written comment indicated a lack of understanding of the meaning of the questions. These were, after all, very concrete questions.

<u>Built-in "Lie Tests"</u>. In the Minnesota Multiphasic Personality Inventory (MMPI) full form of 566 true or false questions, a "lie scale" exists, comparing responses to similar questions appearing in different places on the form. When someone intentionally engages in deceit, they often forget what they lied about before. Thus, it is possible to identify clear inconsistencies in this way. Similar provisions were adopted for the present research methodology by building such "lie tests" or tests of inconsistency into the survey instrument questions. Thus, like the MMPI once scored, our present survey instrument once analyzed provides the basis for identifying deceptive response patterns -- those that are clearly inconsistent or suggestive of deceptive responses.

The first test is one where we could capture any respondent who was paranoid enough to lie about present age and age at time of first arrest. One of the questions in the survey instrument asks, "At what age were you FIRST arrested for any crime? When I was_____years old". Another item in the survey instrument asks, "How old are you today? I am_____years old." A respondent who would engage in early intentional deceit in a response pattern to the survey instrument could therefore be detected by comparing these two items. Deceitful responses would be evident whenever the value of the age for first arrest exceeded the value of present age. A simple computer check allowed for direct testing of this type of systematic deception. Or, for another example, a deceptive respondent might give the age of 17 for current age and give the age of 20 for age at time of first being forced to have sex later in the item order of the survey instrument. The results of this test were that no detected deception of this blatant nature was found.

Several other hypotheses were tested to evaluate the validity of the data. These consisted of matched-pair items that were very similar in nature, that is, the questions basically asked the same thing but the item phraseology was slightly altered. Most of these matched pair variables measuring the same thing were intermixed throughout the survey. By using contingency table or cross-tabulation analysis, the relationship between these paired variables had better be statistically significant by the Chi-square test, because one variable should not significantly differ from a second similar variable if the respondents are being honest with us. We found these tests very significant, with Chi-square values reaching very strong levels. Had these matched-pair lie tests not been significant, then we would have had to conclude that large-scale lie behavior threatened the validity of the data.

A related type of validity test is that of internal consistency in terms of logically expected results. If the expected internal logical consistency is above 95 percent, then that could be considered a measure of the rigor of the methodology in a very large national sample. We can illustrate this with Table 1. Table 1 uses two different questions from the Project GANGFACT survey. The logic here should be obvious in regard to these items. Where a sample of N = 7857 responses were available, what we find here is that only 4.8 percent of the responses are inconsistent with the logical expectation of internal consistency.

Table 1
The Distribution (N) of Belief in God by Being on the Side of God or Satan

Which best describes you:	Which Side Are You On?	
	God's Side	Satan's Side
I BELIEVE IN GOD	7588	241
I DO NOT BELIEVE IN GOD	153	236

Chi-square = 2248.0, p < .001

As in Table 1, a check on internal logical consistency can be made in the overall sample through cross-tabulation of two similar items. The "inconsistency" in Table 1 would be anyone who claims to believe in God but then indicates they are on Satan's side, as well as anyone who claims to not believe in God who then claims to be on God's side. We would not want to argue that generally, in the offender population, anyone is going to always get the full truth about anything. But the "inconsistency" in Table 1 accounts for only 4.7 percent of the sample. This inconsistency is remarkably low given the large sample size (N = 8218) for this test.

In short, much attention in this research during the instrumentation phase was paid to the matter of structuring a variety of opportunities for the respondent to be deceptive or deceitful in a way that could be easily detected by data analysis. We know it is not customary for researchers investigating such offender populations as included in the present research to do this, but we felt that it was necessary to speak to this issue in as much as this was a large scale investigation involving an assortment of known offender groups.

OTHER ISSUES OF VALIDITY

As previously alluded to, much attention to detail and many precautions were undertaken during the research process that were designed to enhance validity by protecting against threats to validity. Additional protective measures that we used will be described here. Overall, we conclude that the validity of the research is higher than average for social research of the type we conducted.

We begin by recognizing that generally in social research, and all criminal justice or criminological research, the term validity is defined as the extent to which the researchers have measured what they purport to measure. Therefore, the ultimate assessment of validity goes directly to the issue of whether or not the survey instrument captures and effectively differentiates the population at-risk for joining gangs, whether it can effectively identify sub-groupings within the gang population (i.e., specific gangs), and whether the questions about gang life, economic issues, and other related factors or variables really measure what they say they measure. We note that the ambiguity in language in the survey instrument was reduced during a field or pretest of the survey instrument. We further note that there were few respondents who did not understand the questions in the survey that they were predicted to understand.

Obviously, we did not assume that non-gang members would understand much about the detailed dynamics of the economic infrastructure and financial aspects of gang life. We did, however, predict that gang members would both understand the meaning of such questions and be able to report their experience and beliefs about these specific aspects of gang life. We therefore report that in terms of the construct validity of the survey instrument itself, gang members clearly did understand and had little difficulty in providing responses to the more than 100 variables in the survey instrument.

The validity concern about of the length of the survey is a moot issue, we feel. Our survey instrument is long, but it can generally be completed in about 30 minutes by most respondents. The structure of the social settings in which the data were collected was such that no "pressure" existed to rapidly complete the questionnaires. The respondents in all social contexts had more time available to them than was needed for the actual completion of the anonymous questionnaire. Normally, about an hour was set aside, and few needed this much time. In some settings, the respondent could take as much time as needed. Thus, by the nature of the precautions taken during the implementation of the research, we rule out any fatigue or "length of survey deterioration" factor as a threat to the validity of this research.

Concurrent criterion validity means examining a measurement in relationship to some other variable it should be highly predictive of. The most important aspect of the current research was defining who was or who was not a gang member. The way in which validity controls were implemented in the present research design therefore asked different versions of the same question for several variables. This also meant being able to induce a high level of quality control: for example, making sure that someone who in one question reports they have ever joined a gang, and who in another variable indicates the exact name of the gang in an open-ended "fill in the blank" type of question (i.e., "What gang did or do you belong to?_____), then indicates the type of alliance or nation status. Thus, any "Gangster Disciple" would, in our sample, have to also indicate a membership in the "Folks" nation. We found very little discrepancy between such variables, and therefore believe that our basic measures that differentiate gang members and non-gang members are very accurate. These are also, for the most part, "brand name" gangs: gangs common to the social contexts from which they were sampled (Crips, Bloods, and Sureno sets on the west coast, etc).

One of the ways in which we were able to use a "criterion" validity approach was our access to probably the best and most current national directory of gangs in America today --- the National Geographic Guide to Gangs in the United States. This is a large computer file maintained by the National Gang Crime Research Center. It is updated from numerous sources (law enforcement, corrections, etc.) every year and has monitored the gang proliferation problem for five years in a row. For a sample listing of this information which is useful in validating gang names for gang members, see the companion volume to An Introduction to Gangs (3rd and expanded edition, 1995): National Gang Resource Handbook: An Encyclopedic Reference (1995, Bristol, Indiana: Wyndham Hall Press). Thus, official sources providing names of numerous gangs in America were used to cross-check the self-disclosed data from respondents in the present research. As the analysis will reveal, the gang members in the present study are, for the most part, in very well known gangs. Thus, for our most important variable of focus (gang membership), we were able to ascertain the validity of the self-reported gang membership by examining it in relationship to other validity control items (name of gang, gang nation alliance, type of rank held in the gang, etc.). We did not encounter any cases that were impostors; for example, only a gang member in a particular gang would know the type of leadership positions in its unique hierarchy.

The present research can rule out a threat to the internal validity of the design based on history. The reason this is true is that all the data were collected in a short period of time during 1996 (spring to fall, 1996), covering about a six month period. The hidden benefit of not being a federally funded research project is that there were few, if any, obstructions to the research process, and the results could be reported in a relatively short time frame as well. Thus, the findings are very much reflective of the current social reality (i.e., we did not have to wait a couple of years to report our findings). For the same reasons, maturation was not a threat to the validity of our research design, because as stated, all data collection occurred in a short period of time nationally in all sites, sometimes simultaneously.

The issue of testing as a threat to validity is common to all surveys on known offenders and all self-report surveys in general. Completing surveys in some of the contexts was a common expectation, particularly among students and youths in juvenile correctional settings. Even the jail inmates have a great deal of experience in completing such questionnaires and "surveys". A number of precautions were taken to ensure the validity of the research design by always having researchers on-site during all data collection; typically, several members of the larger team were present to assist with data collection. Mostly this involved explaining to the potential respondents that this was a completely anonymous survey, it did ask very personal questions and that was the reason we did not want anyone's name, and that the "we" consisted of mostly university professors.

Wherever possible, we tried to off-set the disruption of having unknown persons intruding on their social contexts distributing surveys and pencils by offering some type of consumable amenity as a small reward or honorarium for completing the questionnaire. Thus, in most contexts this was viewed as a pleasant distraction. For these and other reasons already discussed, we do not feel that testing was a major threat to the validity of the present research.

As discussed above as well, the pre-testing or field testing of the survey instrument was designed to eliminate any ambiguity in words, phraseology, expressions, and writing. No respondents were used from the pre-testing. The national sample of gang members was selected after the pre-testing. These are forced-choice questions that are not double-barreled questions; they are pinpointed to specific issues or measurements of background and behavioral experience, beliefs, and attitudes. We posit that the validity of the present study is, therefore, acceptable for studies of its kind regarding any threat to validity from instrumentation. Another reason that we can rule out instrumentation as a major threat to the validity of our research is that a number of our variables are direct replications of those used in previous research found to be acceptable and reported in the literature; where applicable, such literature is specifically cited in the full report.

One of the strengths of the present research regarding validity is how we overcame the potential threat to validity from differential selection of subjects. In gang research, as is common in criminal justice and criminological research on offenders generally, the common situation is to have only one social context in which to study the human aspect of interest. In the present research, as explained earlier, the plan in advance was to develop and use multiple social contexts for data collection. Thus, gang members were studied in a large number of social contexts where we could reasonably assume we could find them: in adult correctional settings, in juvenile correctional settings, in community programs, in probation caseloads, work release centers, boot camps, etc. Further, the geographic representation of the sample was intentional so that we could examine variations across a large span of the United States, including data collection sites in the west (northern and southern California), in the north (North Dakota, Minnesota, Wisconsin), the midwest (Indiana, Iowa, Illinois, Ohio, etc.), the south (Texas, Mississippi, Tennessee, etc.), and the east coast (Massachusetts, New Jersey, Florida, North Carolina, Georgia). A complete list of states is provided in the site cross-reference table (Figure 1). Therefore, in a comparative assessment, our present research is stronger than most in regard to taking precautionary measures to minimize the threat to validity in terms of <u>differential selection of subjects</u> by including a broad cross-section (i.e., across different social contexts) and geographical spectrum of respondents. Our analysis can, therefore, speak to issues of comparison not available in much previous gang research (i.e., comparing west coast Crips/Bloods with midwest People/ Folks, etc).

The issue of <u>mortality</u> for validity is of minimal concern to the present study and is, therefore, not a major threat. This was, after all, a "snapshot" survey design. We only sought out a cross-section of data; this was a multi-state, multi-context, cross-sectional survey research design. It was not intended to be a longitudinal design with follow-up measurements. The only way in which <u>mortality</u> might negatively impact the research design would be if our sampling was limited to only one type of social context, or if we only used one site for each type of social context. The fact is we used multiple social contexts, and for some of these (i.e., jails, juvenile correctional facilities) we used multiple sites within these social contexts as well. Thus, if someone "missed out" from such a site, chances are minimal that we would not be able to still capture the social reality of these social contexts. After all, within the specific social context sites, the research plan called for a "saturation" sampling method: everyone in the jail, the prison, the juvenile center, etc., was asked to complete the questionnaire. Very few persons refused to complete the questionnaire. We tried to structure our data collection in correctional settings so that we did not interfere with court calls or visiting. Consequently, we often had to be at the jail late at night on some occasions, and almost always on the weekends, requiring travel and overnight stays in various cities for some of the researchers. Through previous research experience, the researchers knew how to structure the data collection process to be minimally disruptive to the security and other concerns of correctional facilities. We do know that with a long survey instrument such as that used in the present research project, there may be "item mortality." That is not a matter of "attention deficit disorders," it is a matter of simply losing the respondent at some later point in the survey instrument, resulting in some cases missing data for those items towards the end of the survey instrument.

The present research is, therefore, not unlike other similar survey research designs in having the common problem of some missing data on the many variables measured.

Finally, the issue of <u>regression</u> as a threat to validity is viewed as minimal in the present research. Measurement error was not a major problem, given the fact that among gang members our variables designed to elicit the nature of their economic experiences in and associated with gang life were questions or items or variables that are both replicable and have little, if any, ambiguity. No cognitive bias exists in regard to the variables used in the research. We did not simply include extreme cases, such as those highly cooperative youths on a street corner who might suddenly become very interested in a research project when a person of higher social class and social power arrives on the scene to offer aid and assistance --- material and psychological. The fact is our gang analysis covers the complete gang risk continuum, as the analysis will reveal.

The gang member respondent was particularly prone to write lengthy and unsolicited comments in the margins of the surveys. This highly affective arousal signaled clearly that the respondents understood <u>all too well</u> the meaning of the questions. Sometimes this running commentary of unsolicited remarks directed feedback to the researchers in various ways, explaining subtle nuances, some of which are discussed in the full report at appropriate points in the presentation of results. These were questions that gang members clearly understood, enough so that often such members would strike up conversations and seek out attention from the researchers at almost all the sites. The typical gang member respondent was very curious that anyone would ask such specific questions about gang life today. Thus, it was not uncommon for the researchers to stay around the site for additional time to answer direct questions from the youths; this was particularly true in the juvenile correctional settings.

To recap, in regard to many of the common threats to the internal validity of research such as that reported here (history, maturation, testing, instrumentation, differential selection of subjects, experimental mortality, statistical regression), the precautions taken in the research design and the scope and extent of the research effort (i.e., covering several states, different social contexts, and a large sample) render these threats as minimal.

RELIABILITY

The issue of reliability is the matter of the "quality" of the data. The informed reader will recognize that the term reliability in research means basically, "do we get the same results with repeated measures?" Over time it is possible, indeed probable, that "gang life" and the gang problem can, could and might change. For example, the gang problem has expanded and proliferated in recent years in the United States. In another sense, the meaning of <u>reliability</u> in the type of social research conducted here often means "would different researchers going to the same places using the same questions get the same results?" We argue, by the nature of the methodological rigor and level of effort in the present research design, that this would, in fact, be the case to a high degree. In other words, when we issue what are called "site reports," or rapid information summaries back to the host sites that provided access for data collection, our data truly does reflect the social reality of their environment. Most who have received these site reports agree with us in regard to the critical issues, specifically, gang density and the scope and extent of the gang member problem in their populations.

This is not to say that the problem may not escalate or deteriorate in the years ahead. The nature of our research purpose is not to predict the future. Rather, our intent is limited by the nature of our research methodology --- a cross-sectional survey design using large samples --- to simply describing the current situation in these various social contexts. Given the rapid feedback, that is little time delay between data collection and the reporting of findings, we also argue that our research has high reliability in terms of the volatility of such data: ours was recently collected and quickly reported. Our generalizations are to the present, not the future, as we recognize the gang problem is a dynamic and not a static problem. But the trained researcher will also recognize that the methodological matter of reliability is really the simple and testable issue of whether the same measurement techniques used in different research settings or at different points in time produce the same results. We can give and test an example of this aspect of reliability. Different questions at different points in the item order of the survey produced almost identical results.

However, if this instrument is lacking in the area of reliability, it would become obvious if multiple sites were chosen to study the issues of gang prevention and gang intervention. That is, the hypothesis of logical inference is that in the same city, among members of the same gangs, there should be no difference in the responses if we asked the same questions in different social settings -- indeed, social settings that are mutually exclusive.

Our research was structured in a way to enhance both validity and reliability. Thus, in some jurisdictions we surveyed all facilities that existed in the area. For example, the study included all juvenile correctional institutions in the State of Ohio, most of the prisons in North Carolina, and all juvenile correctional facilities, short- and long-term, in the State of Tennessee. Thus, in different geographical areas we had sites that were in some respects representing the "universe" of that particular state. As correctional inmate research goes, there are few studies that exceed the level of effort represented in the present project.

As there were many researchers in 17 states carrying out the same type of data collection in similar types of facilities (jails, prisons, juvenile institutions, etc.), to enhance reliability the project required a standardized presentation when meeting directly for the first time with the confined population. This standardized presentation explained that it was a national project, that a variety of researchers were associated with various universities and other groups, and that no names were needed; it was a completely anonymous survey. The researchers on-site collected the surveys directly from the inmates. The researchers in most cases also directly handed out rewards to the inmates for their cooperation.

OTHER ISSUES OF VALIDITY AND RELIABILITY: FOR IMPROVING FUTURE RESEARCH

No replication problems materialized in the present research, as many of the variables or items (i.e., survey questions) had been used and reported in the prior literature. However, in the few instances where new variables were used, such as questions on the economic life of gangs and other factors included in some of the sites (i.e., sexual abuse, family life, etc.) in this comprehensive survey, we felt that some improvements could be made in terms of the structure of such questions. These recommendations appear in the presentation of results and in their interpretation at relevant points in the full report. We also provide suggestions for improving the validity and reliability of these measurements for purposes of future research. We recognize that there is no such thing as the "perfect" model of social research on anything, but improvements can always be made.

TYPES OF GANGS REPRESENTED IN THE SAMPLE OF OVER 4,000 GANG MEMBERS

The full list of gangs represented in this large national sample includes several hundred different gangs, most of whom fall into the Crips, Blood, People, and Folks classification system. This sample includes over 200 members of the Gangster Disciples gang in Chicago, for example. A large variety of sets of Crips and Bloods are represented in the sample as well. The types of gangs cut across the ethnic and racial spectrum as well (white, Black, Latino, Asian). The gangs represented are, for the most part, the more serious types of gangs of interest to the criminological researcher. In addition to the gangs mentioned above, other gangs that are represented include the Aryan Brotherhood, a variety of factions of Vice Lords from the midwestern United States (Insane Vice Lords, Conservative Vice Lords, Unknown Vice Lords, Mafia Insane Vice Lords, Traveller Vice Lords) and literally all types of disciples (Gangster Disciples, Black Disciples, Maniac Latin Disciples, etc.).

WHY WE KNOW THE GANG MEMBERS ARE IN THE GANGS THEY PURPORT TO BE MEMBERS OF

For most of the sites used in Project GANGFACT we used a unique methodological tool developed by the National Gang Crime Research Center. It involves a comparison of the symbols, logos, signs and expressions known to be used by the gang a person purports to be a member of. Respondents who reported that they were members of a gang were asked at the end to draw a picture of some of the gang's signs, symbols, logos, graffiti, etc. This was one of our additional validity control devices.

SUMMARY
    In this chapter we have provided full details about the research methodology. Given the attention to detail regarding validity and reliability, and the large size of the national sample developed, the authors assert that the methodological rigor gives this study strong grounding. We conclude that the validity and reliability of the data are acceptable for surveys of this type and nature.

FIGURE 1
TYPE OF SOCIAL CONTEXT BY SIZE OF GANG SAMPLE
Self-Reported Gang Member?

	Missing	NO	YES	Total
Louisiana Training Institute	4	40	39	83
Rivarde Training Inst. (Louisiana))	2	20	25	47
Florida Parish Detention Center (Louisiana)	1	11	13	25
Monmouth Co. Jail (New Jersey)	5	147	54	206
Dade Metro Juvenile Detention Center (Miami, Florida)	5	110	48	163
Stockton, California (Juvenile Center)	1	21	23	45
Indian River Juvenile Correctional Center (Ohio)	13	159	133	305
Riverside Juvenile Correctional Center (Ohio)	5	97	66	168
DeKalb County Jail (Illinois)	2	28	6	36

Figure 1: Continued
Self-Reported Gang Member?

	Missing	NO	YES	Total
Lincoln Hills Juven. Correctional Center (Wisconsin)	6	77	199	282
Augusta Juvenile Correctional Inst. (Georgia)	21	115	96	232
Texas Boot Camp	2	1	46	49
Macon Georgia Female Juvenile Corr'l. Institution.	3	97	54	154
Milledgeville Juv. Corr. Inst. GEORGIA	9	164	141	314
Lake County, Indiana Juvenile Detention Center	4	19	42	65
Sciotto State Juv. Corr. Inst. OHIO	18	27	83	128
Cuyahoga Juv. Corr. Inst. OHIO	14	157	147	318
TICO, Juv. Corr. Institution, OHIO	31	132	103	266
Atlanta, GA Male YDC GEORGIA	7	88	41	136
Foothills Main Corr'l. Facility NORTH CAROLINA	7	152	129	288
Audy Home: Chicago Cook County Temporary Juvenile Det. Center	17	124	429	570

Figure 1: Continued
Self-Reported Gang Member?

	Missing	NO	YES	Total
Scott Co. Jail IOWA	5	117	45	167
Foothills Camp NORTH CAROLINA	23	97	43	163
Central Prison NORTH CAROLINA	5	86	32	123
Juvenile Residential Programs in ND and MN	1	37	39	77
Parchman Prison Parchman, Mississippi	31	257	52	340
Fresno, California Juv. Det. Center	0	19	88	107
Woodland Hills Youth Dev. Ctr. TENNESSEEE	4	66	49	119
Circleville Juv. Corr. Institution OHIO	9	89	65	163
Mohican Village Juv. Corr. Inst. OHIO	3	79	85	167
Maumee Juv. Corr'l. Inst. OHIO	1	72	52	125
Chatauga Corr'l. Center NORTH CAROLINA	0	28	4	32
Metro Detention Facility CCA Nashville. TENN.	22	285	71	378

Figure 1: Continued
Self-Reported Gang Member?

	Missing	NO	YES	Total
Paint Creek Juv. Corr. Center OHIO	2	15	16	33
Cook County Jail Chicago, ILLINOIS	39	195	182	416
Tenn. Women's Prison	6	196	15	217
Rutherford Co. Jail Tennessee	3	130	23	156
Nashville City Jail CJC Tennessee	20	233	39	292
McLean Co. Jail ILLINOIS	4	96	57	157
State Female Prison Texas	0	14	17	31
S. Texas Co. Jail	0	27	9	36
HD1 and HD2 Jail Units Nashville, Tennessee	2	144	29	175
Greene Corr'l. Center North Carolina	3	73	20	96
New Hanover Corr'l. Ctr. NORTH CAROLINA	0	24	16	40
Sandhills Youth Inst. North Carolina	0	18	17	35
Harnett Corr'l. Ctr. North Carolina	4	114	29	147
Wayne Corr'l. Center North Carolina	1	38	12	51

Figure 1: Continued
Self-Reported Gang Member?

	Missing	NO	YES	Total
Franklin Corr'l. Center North Carolina	4	77	23	104
Sanford Corr'l. Center North Carolina	1	7	5	13
N.C.C.I.W. (NC25) North Carolina	3	91	15	109
Piedmont Corr'l Ctr. North Carolina	5	63	15	83
NC07 Polk Corr'l Inst. North Carolina	10	79	48	137
Johnston Corr'l Inst. North Carolina	4	32	5	41
Durham Corr'l. Ctr. North Carolina	5	22	10	37
Davidson Co. Juvenile Det. Center Nashville, TN	0	15	12	27
Youth Development Ctr. Sommerville, Tenn.	0	54	66	120
Mountain View YDC Dandridge, Tenn.	0	57	63	120
Taft Y.D.C. Pikeville, Tennessee	10	52	53	115
Work Release Ctr. and DUI Center, Nashville, Tennessee	4	113	17	134
Shelby Co. Juven. Det. Center Memphis, TENN	6	63	25	94

	Figure 1: Continued			
	Self-Reported Gang Member?			
	Missing	NO	YES	Total
Tulare Co. Juv. Det. Center Tulare Co., California	0	7	45	52
Caucteret Corr.Ctr. North Carolina	5	56	17	78
Rutherford Co. Juv. Det. Center Murfreesboro, Tenn.	3	12	10	25
St Bernard's Parish Juv. Det. Center Louisiana	0	5	5	10
Hampden Co.Corr'l Center, Ludlow, Mass.	1	3	5	9
NC37, Eastern Corr'l Inst., North Carolina	0	14	1	15
Independence Hall, Juv. Facility, Ohio	2	8	12	22
Freedom Center, OHIO	1	12	4	17
NC19, Vance Corr'l Center, N. Carolina	0	3	1	4
NC20, Umstead Corr'l Center, N. Carolina	2	6	3	11
NC21, Warren Corr'l Inst., N. Carolina	1	18	3	22
NC16, Person Corr'l Center, N. Carolina	0	4	4	8
NC15, Orange Corr'l Center, N. Carolina	0	0	3	3
NC27, Black Mountain Corr'l Ctr. For Women N. Carolina	1	21	0	22

Figure 1: Continued
Self-Reported Gang Member?

	Missing	NO	YES	Total
NC26, Raleigh Corr'l Center for Women N. Carolina	0	14	1	15
NC28, Wilmington RFW (Halfway House) N. Carolina	0	7	1	8
NC35, Martin Corr'l Center, N. Carolina	0	4	3	7
NC12, Halifax Corr'l Center, N. Carolina	0	10	2	12
NC13, Granville Corr'l Center, N. Carolina	0	2	0	2
Co. Jail in Texas	1	31	10	42
Jail Lock-up in Texas	0	3	19	22
State Corr'l Facility Texas	1	41	16	58
Juvenile Halfway House Texas	2	25	13	40
Central Juvenile Hall Los Angeles, California	4	107	286	397
Los Padrinas Juv. Hall Downey, California	0	112	296	408

TOTAL MISSING   441

TOTAL NO   5,585

TOTAL YES   4,140

TOTAL N   10.166

CHAPTER THREE

BULLYING BEHAVIOR: AN INVASION ON OUR SCHOOLS

Shirley R. Holmes, Ph.D.
North Georgia College and State University

INTRODUCTION

An alarming trend in the lifestyle of our youth today is the rapid rise of violence in schools! Many of our youth seem to be preoccupied with anger, destruction and violence. Their activities have been well documented to include car jacking, fighting, selling drugs, drive-by shootings and murder (Knox, 1994). Today's youth are armed with weapons (guns), which are usually of a higher caliber than the weapons used by police. And, they do not think twice about using their weapons to obtain what they call security, power, self-respect and fun. As a result, they appear fearless to danger, arrest or incarceration.

The Federal Bureau of Investigation (FBI) has reported that arrests of youth for violent crimes decreased three percent in 1995 and six percent in 1996, following a steady increase throughout the late 1980s and early 1990s. Even so, the number of arrests of youths for violent crimes in 1996 was 60 percent higher than in 1987 (Snyder, 1997). To be specific, from 1987 to 1996, arrests of juveniles for rape decreased three percent, but arrests of youths for murder, robbery and aggravated assault increased 50, 57 and 70 percent respectively. On the other hand, from 1992 to 1996, juvenile arrests for murder decreased 18 percent and rape arrests decreased seven percent, while arrests for robbery increased seven percent and arrests for aggravated assault increased two percent. And from 1995 to 1996, juvenile arrests for murder decreased another 14 percent, robbery arrests decreased eight percent, arrests for aggravated assault decreased four percent, and rape arrests remained stable. Despite the evidence that juvenile arrests for violent crimes have leveled-off or declined, violent activities in schools have increased (Rutherford & Nelson, 1995).

Researchers have reported that the majority of our schools are plagued with youth crime, including aggressive behavior. Violations range from breaking school rules to the use of weapons in school (Shanker, 1995; Goldstein & Conoley, 1997). Classroom teachers have expressed that they have been observing more school violence today than yesterday, but violence in a different form - bullying (Holmes & Ayres, 1998).

Bullying appears to be a pervasive and growing problem throughout the schools. Hawkins (1996) found school bullying to be on the rise and escalating throughout school systems, including high school, middle school, elementary and preschool. According to Hazler (1994), this type of behavior (bullying) has caused more fear, suffering, school dropouts, suicides and murder among our youth than any other behavior in school. Meanwhile, Lane (1989) noted that school bullying was rarely on the school agenda and had received relatively little attention from the national or the local authorities, including the teacher's union.

Bullying in school deserves substantially greater attention than it has received in the past. When bullying is practiced in a forceful manner, it could develop into a critical issue at any grade level. Such behaviors usually surface before the student becomes a "wannabe" or "gangbanger," thus indicating that bullying could be the precursor, the beginning stage or the stepping stone to gang involvement and other delinquent acts. Wilson and Petersilia (1995) viewed such behaviors as the foundation upon which more serious youth violence rests. Regarding the latter, it appears urgent that educators become aware of the various signs, activities and interventions associated with bullying in school, which is the main purpose of this chapter.

This chapter explores the various issues related to the phenomenon of bullying behaviors among school children, along with the characteristics and common features of both the bully and the victim. This chapter will also present current data collected from self-reported gang members pertaining to bullying behaviors in school - Project GANGFACT. And, in conclusion, this chapter offers a variety of suggestions for the curtailment of bullying in school and in the classroom.

BACKGROUND

The phenomenon of school bullying is not new. For years, bullying behaviors were considered a part of growing up, petty teasing, joking around, harmless fun or kids being kids (Holmes, 1997). The fact that some children are humiliated, teased and attacked by other children in school has probably been around as long as children have been going to school.

Numerous examples and writings about school children bullying other school children have been described in literature since the mid 1800's (Olweus,

1993). Around 1850, Thomas Hughes, author of the English novel, *Tom Brown's School Days*, provides an example of early school bullying. He described older boys daily picking on younger boys, e.g. knocking their books down, tripping them in the halls, and pushing them around. Later in the year, the older boys would force the younger boys to undergo sadistic roasting in front of an open fire - "just for fun" (Greenbaum, Garrison, James & Stephens, 1989).

During the early 1970's, bullying appeared to be more 'silly acting" than harmful among school children. Many children joked around with each other in laughter, with maybe some teasing, "horse-playing" or name-calling. This behavior has changed!

School bullying today appears to encompass a variety of violent aggressive behaviors with activities committed by youngsters on youngsters with the intent to hurt the other person. The changes in bullying we see today in comparison to yesterday include an increase in the frequency of the behavior (daily), the intent to hurt the other person (more aggressive behavior), and the use of weapons, particularly guns (Holmes, 1997). So what is bullying behavior?

DEFINITION
Bullying behavior involves a continuum of behaviors including name calling, intimidation, extortion or fighting (Mooney, Creaser, & Bletchford, 1991), and an unprovoked and deliberate intention to hurt with repeated negative assaults (Slee, 1993).
Bullying is also defined as an imbalance of strength, either physical or psychological, with negative, aggressive behaviors directed toward the other person (Olweus, 1987).

It is important to note that many bullies do not display all of the behaviors mentioned in the various definitions. Some bullies may daily tease, or constantly humiliate, or repeatedly attack their victims, whereas other bullies may use a combination of all the above behaviors, with or without violence. Whatever means of operation or degree of intensity bullies may practice, any type or style of bullying should be considered inappropriate behavior both in and out of school.

Researchers have given several definitions of behaviors considered school bullying. These various definitions may cause problems in identifying what behaviors are bullying and what behaviors are "rough" playing. With this thought in mind, researchers have revealed some common features among bullies that may help in identifying bullying behaviors.

COMMON FEATURES AMONG BULLIES
According to Hoover and Hazler (1991), one distinct common feature of bullies is the constant use of aggressive behaviors toward others. This type of behavior could be verbal, which may include teasing, name-calling, cursing and/or racial slurs. The behavior could also be physical, such as fighting, taking another's property and/or physically harassing another, usu-

ally with violence. It appears that bullies have a fascination with violence, which they utilize to obtain their goal – power.

Another common feature of bullies is the strong need to dominate others (Olweus, 1994). Bullies appear to have little empathy for their victims and will often do whatever it takes to subdue the victim to accomplish their dominance. Bjorkqvist, Ekman and Largerspetz (1982) expressed that bullies who had a strong need to dominate others were constantly and consistently inflicting fear, injury and bodily harm upon their victim(s). Bandura (1973) indicated that this type of behavior was a form of prestige among bullies. Jensen and Yerington (1997) implied that this type of behavior could be the bully's way of looking powerful or important to their peers.

Still another common feature among bullies is their intense need for control over others and situations (Slee, 1993; Stephenson & Smith, 1989). These are the children who always have to be first in line and in the games they play. They usually tell everyone else what part they will play and they usually make up the rules to ensure that they will win. The difference between playing with a spoiled child versus a bully is the bully's means of obtaining such control. Bullies will demand control through constant verbal and physical abuse, which often includes intimidation, harassment and hitting. The spoiled child will not use such means. Webster (1991) noted that bullies who used abusive means for controlling others were relieving their own feelings of inadequacies, insecurities, and/or poor self-esteem. However, other research has not supported this latter point of view, but rather has shown results that pointed in the opposite direction (Olweus, 1993). Pulkkinen and Tremblay's (1992) study found that bullies had little insecurities and were not suffering from poor self-esteem.

And lastly, a common feature among bullies seems to be their ability to seek out and stalk their victim before engaging in bullying behavior. They carefully stalk the student who is physically weak, has low self-esteem, is isolated from others and/or attends special education classes (Hoover & Hazler, 1991). They also seek the student who is either overweight, has red hair, wears glasses, or who speaks in a "mannerable way" (Hoover & Juul, 1993; Olweus, 1994). Bullies usually do not pick on or intimidate just anyone indiscriminately, but look for the student who is considered different, veers from the standards, and most of all, will not fight back.

Features of a bully could be described as an underlying pattern of interrelated motives. First, bullies seem to use aggressive behaviors, such as constant intimidation, harassment, and violence as tools to obtain their goals – power and control. And second, bullies seem to need these tools of aggressive behaviors to inflict fear, pain and suffering upon others to maintain their goals. But, what about the victims?

COMMON FEATURES OF VICTIMS

In contrast to the research devoted to understanding the common features of the bully, very little is known about the features of the victims. Research has indicated that there are two known categories of victims - "passive" and "provocative" (Garrity, Jens, Porter, Sager & Camilli, 1997). According to Garrity et al (1997), the passive victim will not fight back, verbally or physically. They usually give in or yield to the demands of the bully. They are often considered anxious, insecure and lack the social skills needed for integrating socially with other children. Hoover and Hazler (1991) noted these features among some students in special education classes who were also victims of bullies. They concluded that these victims did lack integrative social skills due to their isolation in special education classes (e.g. Learning Disabilities). Therefore, such placement should be considered a compounding feature for these children.

Passive victims usually have their own way of coping with bullies. Some victims may cry easily when confronted by bullies, whereas other victims may isolate themselves or hide so as not to be confronted by bullies. Others may give in to the bullies because of their inadequacies, physical weakness, or past abuse. Needless to say, these are the features that often make the passive victim an easy prey for the bully.

The other category of victims is often referred to as the provocative victim because of his/her behavior (Garrity, et al, 1997). Their behavior may consist of purposely stirring-up trouble, inciting anger and/or causing agitation among other students, including the bullies in the school. Unlike the passive victim, the provocative victim will not isolate him/herself, nor run in fear of the bullies. And contrary to popular belief, the provocative victim will fight back, verbally and physically, when confronted. Although the provocative victim will stand up for him/herself, may incite some conflicting situations and will usually fight back, he/she is not a match for the bully. The provocative victim will usually lose the fight and the power struggle with the bully.

Some researchers have indicated that most provocative victims suffer from Attention Deficit Hyperactive Disorder (ADHD) or Emotional/Behavioral Disorder (E/BD) (Garrity, et al, 1997; Whelan, 1988). Their behavioral characteristics appear very similar to children with ADHD or E/BD. For example, the provocative victim is usually: 1. quick to lose control in various situations; 2. easy to emotionally arouse about most things; 3. very restless for the majority of the time; 4. irritated constantly; and 5. can not handle frustrations, stress, or disappointments.

The above behavior characteristics of the provocative victim may appear like the behavior of bullies. But in reality, the behaviors are different. If one would look closely at the motives of the provocative victim and the bully, one may find three possible behavioral differences: 1. bullies usually try to hurt the other student, whereas provocative victims are not out to hurt anyone; 2. bullies engage in daily negative behaviors toward other students, but provocative victims do not engage in "daily" negative behaviors; and

3. where bullies pick on other students who are weak or different from most students, provocative victims do not selectively pick on other students - they just annoy everybody. Needless to say, provocative victims are still targets for the bully.

Many students, passive or provocative, often suffer in silence. They usually believe that the problem is their fault and they deserve what is happening to them. Some believe that if they looked prettier, if they were smarter, if they could act differently, etc., then this would not happen to them. They tend to feel helpless and hopeless over the situation; therefore, they do not expect help. These are the children who usually do not tell their parents or the teacher about being bullied at school.

Only recently have we come to recognize the early signs of a bully or victim in school. Troy and Scoufe (1987) found children 4-7 years old displaying various aggressive behaviors towards their playmates, including kicking, biting, teasing, name calling and fighting - possible signs of bullying. John and Carr (1995) reported that they observed two incidents of school bullying and victimization in a kindergarten class. One incident was the verbal demand of one youngster to another to give him the toy he was playing with or he would "beat him up." Needless to say, the youngster gave him the toy - the sign of a passive victim. Another incident, in the same kindergarten classroom, involved the physical attack of one youngster upon his classmate because he wanted his place in line. The two youngsters got into a physical fight about the demand; however, the victim lost the fight and his place in line - the sign of a provocative victim.

Bullying behavior and victimization have also been observed among middle and high school students (Maloney, 1995). The demand of money, the taking of property (e.g. clothing, pencils, notebooks), the daily name calling, the constant put downs, and in some situations the physical fighting, with or without weapons, are only a few of the bullying behaviors among older students.

Youth who have been victimized over a long period of time often suffer from low self-esteem, constant fear of others and low academic performance (Barr & Parrett, 1995). Some victims may drop out of school and later develop a lack of trust in people which could carry over into their adult lives (Bornfield, 1987).

Bullying behavior can be a devastating experience for most victims and bullies. The results of bullying can scar the victim for life. In extreme cases, it may cause the victim to arm himself/herself and fatally wound his/her tormentors and other classmates (Fox 5, Eyewitness News, 1997), or the victim may commit suicide to stop the torment (Manning & Baruth, 1995; Osofsky, 1997). The results of bullying can also scar the bully for life, as it may lead him/her into a world of crime and incarceration for the rest of his/her life (Knox, et al., 1997).

The above findings are only a few of the reasons why it is so important for educators to identify problem behaviors (bullying) in early childhood development. However, researchers have found that many of the behaviors are often missed or ignored by educators and parents. The following studies may explain their findings.

STUDIES

In a study constructed in response to a playground murder, Kelly and Cohn (1988) discovered that 66 percent of the first and fourth grade students in a Manchester school reported being bullies. Interestingly, in the same study, only 16 percent of the teachers identified concerns about physical aggression among their students and verbal aggression was mentioned as a concern of far less importance. In a similar type of study, Hoover, Oliver and Hazler (1992) documented that 66 percent of all students reported that officials responded poorly to incidents of bullying. Slee (1992) reported on the frequency of being bullied. He found that bullying everyday ranged in frequency from 1 percent to 8 percent. Some 10 percent of the children in this study indicated that the teachers "hardly ever" or "never" tried to stop the bullying.

A study of 700 eleven-year-old students found that 26 percent of the mothers were aware that their child was being bullied but indicated that it was not a serious concern (Newson & Newson, 1984). Stevenson and Smith (1989) studied 1,000 fourth grade students and discovered that the teachers identified approximately 25 percent of their students as being involved in bullying behavior, but they thought it was a minor problem.

On a similar investigation, Hoover, Oliver and Hazler (1992) studied bullying identification with 200 mid-western middle and high school students. Seventy-six percent of these students reported that they had been victims of bullying about two or three times per week, but they did not always report the incidents to the teacher. The victims' reasons for lack of reporting such incidents were that "nothing" would be done about it, and the bullies would punish them more harshly for telling the teacher.

Identification of the extent to which bullying occurs in school is difficult. In one study less than 18 percent of <u>witnessed</u> bullying incidents were reported to the staff. Failure of the staff to respond effectively to student complaints of bullying, fear of reprisal by bullies and shame regarding social competence are all factors affecting the low incidence of reports (Slee, 1993; Mooney et al., 1991).

Other factors that emerged as significant descriptors of bullying are attributed to cultural and gender differences. In some cultures studied, teasing is considered more benign or playful, and fighting is regarded as more prevalent (Maccoby, 1986; Maccoby and Jacklin, 1980). Gender differences in studies of bullying have consistently demonstrated that males were more likely to be involved in bullying than females, and they were more likely to be involved in physical aggression (Askew, 1988). Roland (1988) argued that boys involved in bullying were usually doing so as a part of a power-based social relationship, with socialization processes being the key feature of a tolerance for aggressive behaviors.

Females involved in bullying are more likely to be involved in verbal abuse, social isolation, teasing, back-stabbing and popularity contests (Bowers, Smith and Binney, 1994; Mooney, Creaser and Blatchford, 1991; Stepp, 1992).

According to the National Center for Education Statistics, for 1988, girls were less likely to get involved in physical fights. However, during the 1989-90 school year, researchers surveyed 6th - 12th grade students in the United States (about 50,000) and discovered that 45 percent of the girls reported being involved in violent aggressive behavior, compared with 65 percent of the boys (Stepp, 1992). These data indicate that boys and girls have become more similar than ever before in terms of engaging in aggressive behaviors.

Mailk (1990) surveyed 612 secondary school students. One-third of the students reported that they had been bullied in the form of someone calling them nasty names in reference to their skin color or race. According to Whitney and Smith (1993), about 15 percent of students in the junior/middle schools and 9 percent in the secondary schools reported bullying in the form of nasty racial name-calling. They also added that racial name-calling was approximately equal in frequency to physical harm, which may have included being attacked, harassed and/or isolated.

So far, we have discussed various studies of bullying behavior and victims of bullies found in the United States. However, the existence of bully/victim situations found in schools is not confined to the borders of the United States. Research from Munthe (1989) reported that about 5 percent of elementary and secondary school students were regularly bullied going to their school, in school and on their way from school in Scandinavia, and about the same percentage of students were considered bullies. Their bullying activities usually included teasing, name calling and/or isolation.

In Norway, Hoover and Juul (1993) concluded that 9 percent of school children were victims and 7 percent of children were bullies, particularly with an activity known as "mobbing." Heineman (1972) described mobbing as an anonymous group of children or one child engaged in harassing or pestering another. Smith (1991) found that in England over 20 percent of school children were victims and 10 percent were bullies. Their bullying behavior often included name-calling, harassment and physical attacks.

Needless to say, the prevalence of bullying in the United States appears greater than in other countries. Olewus (1984) wrote that American schools "harbor" approximately 2.7 million victims and 2.1 million bullies. Shelly (1985) reported that bullying behavior in the United States occurred at a higher rate and reflected higher levels of overall violence than that found in other countries. He also stated that nearly 80 percent of high school students had reported being bullied during their school career. When United States students were asked about bullying activities, they consistently identified verbal harassment, ridicule, teasing and physical violence as the most common bullying behaviors across ages and sexes (Hoover and Juul, 1993).

It can be argued that bullying behaviors should be directed into constructive activities, starting in early childhood development. If these behaviors are not directed constructively or channeled, the bully may develop negative patterns for achieving goals through threat or actual attack (Elkind and Weiner, 1978). These negative patterns are often displayed throughout life in various types of destructive behavior, possibly including a progression from antisocial behavior to violent behavior, to juvenile delinquency, to gang membership and finally, to adult criminality (Holmes, 1995).

Researchers have estimated that approximately 60 percent of the children characterized as bullies in school have been convicted at least once for a crime before the age of 18 (Albanese, 1994; Olweus, 1994). Others have stated that 35 to 40 percent of former bullies had about three or more convictions by the age of 20; this would include stealing, disruption and fighting (Hawkins, 1996; Holmes, 1995; Knox, 1994). Young adults who were former bullies seem to increase their activity to a level of serious criminality to include carjacking, possession of drugs, weapons, gang membership and murder (School Safety Update, 1994). About 60 percent of these youth are either in prison or dead by the age of 21 (Jensen & Yerington, 1997). The connections between gang membership, aggressive behavior and school bullying are best explained in the study Project GANGFACT (Knox, et al., 1997).

PROJECT GANGFACT

To further investigate the relationship between school bullying, youth violence and gang involvement, we, as members of the National Gang Crime Research Center, conducted an Anonymous National Youth Survey throughout the United States. Part of the study was conducted to determine if there was a significant relationship between bullying in the early years and later gang involvement. The hypothesis was evaluated through data collected from thousands of incarcerated youth as part of a comprehensive study of gangs and violence known as PROJECT GANGFACT. The methodology of this study is described in Chapter 2.

RESULTS

For the purpose of this chapter, the results from the survey will be confined to those questions pertaining to bullying activities in school.

Being Bullied While in School

The survey asked, "Were you ever bullied by anyone in school?" The results showed that 37.5 percent (N=3757) reported that they had been bullied. Over half (62.5 percent, N=6261) reported that they had not been bullied.

Table 1
Incarcerated Youth Who Reported Being Bullied In School

	N	%
No Bullying	6,261	62.5
Experienced Bullying	3,757	37.5
Total	10.018	100.0

Age First Bullied in School

If the person had been bullied while in school, the survey asked the follow-up question: "At what age were you first bullied by someone in your school?" The responses to this question ranged from 5 years old to 21 years old. The mean, or arithmetic average, was 9.7 years of age.

Being a Bully in School

The survey asked: "Did you ever bully someone in school?" About half (47.1 percent, N=4721) said yes, and 52.9 percent (N=5294) said no.

Table 2
Incarcerated Youth Identifying Themselves As Bullies In School

	N	%
Bullied	4,721	47.1
Did Not Bully	5,294	52.9
Total	10,015	100.0

The comparison of gang members and non-gang members on this factor was significant (Chi-square=657.1, p<.001), where 36.1 percent of the non-gang members were bullies, compared with 62.5 percent of the gang members.

Age First Bullied Someone Else in School

If the person had been a bully while in school, the survey asked the follow-up question: "At what age did you first bully someone else in school?" The mean, or arithmetic average, was 11.4 years of age for first bullying someone else in school.

Can Bullying Lead to Gangbanging?

The survey asked: "Do you think bullying in school can lead to gangbanging?" Over two-thirds (70.4 percent, N=6990) of the respondents said yes, while only 29.6 percent (N=2938) said no. The comparison of gang members and non-gang members was not significant.

Female Bullies

Data on females was examined separately. In comparing female non-gang members with female gang members in the confined offender population, the question was asked: " Did you ever bully someone in school?" There was a significant difference (Chi-square=98.1, p< .001) between female gang and non-gang members, with 62.6 percent of gang members saying they had bullied someone versus 30.3 percent of non-gang members.

Table 3
Bullying Behavior Reported By Incarcerated Females -- Gang Members
and Non-Members Of Gang

	Distribution for Incarcerated Females			
	Non-Members		Members of Gangs	
	N	%	N	%
No Bullying	536	69.6	120	37.4
Bullied	234	30.0	201	62.6
Total	770	99.6	321	100.0

Effect of Level of Gang Organization on Bullying

Data were cross-tabulated to determine if the level of social organization of the gang had an effect on bullying. Only the responses of gang members were used for this analysis. For analyzing the level of social organization, the gangs were categorized as either informal or formal based on the responses to another question about gang structure. The survey asked: "Did you ever bully someone in school?"

Table 4
Reports of School Bullying By Level of Gang Organization:
Formal and Informal Groups

	Level of Gang Organization			
	Formal Group		Informal Group	
	N	%	N	%
Bullied	771	69.5	952	62.6
No Bullying	337	30.0	550	37.0
Total	1108	99.5	1502	99.6

The difference between gang members based on level of organization of the gang was significant (Chi-square=13.5, p<.001), with more of those belonging to formal gangs engaging in bullying than those belonging to informal gangs (69.5 percent versus 62.6 percent).

Effect of Level of Organization on Belief That Bullying Leads to Gangbanging

Data were also analyzed to determine whether level of gang organization had an effect on the member's belief that bullying could lead to gangbanging. The difference was significant (Chi-square = 10.3, p = .001), with more members of formal gangs believing that bullying can lead to later gang involvement (73.2 percent versus 67.3 percent).

Table 5
Opinions by Members of Formal and Informal Gangs Regarding Bullying
As A Precursor to Gang Membership

| | Level of Gang Organization | | | |
| | Formal Group | | Informal Group | |
	N	%	N	%
Bullying Does Lead To Gangs	996	67.3	817	73.2
Bullying Does Not Lead To Gangs	483	32.6	299	26.7
Total	1479	99.9	1116	99.9

DISCUSSION

The results of the self-report survey establish bullying as significantly associated with later gang involvement. In addition, those youths involved in gangs with more formal organizational structures were more likely to be bullies than members of less organized gangs. The study further determined that female gang members were significantly more likely than males to have been bullied in school, but just as likely as males to subsequently engage in bullying behavior, supporting previous studies describing gender differences in the development of bullies.

The results of the study support the need for development of proactive intervention with young children at risk for development of bullying behavior as a means of prevention of violent, criminal and gang behavior later in life. The data suggest that individuals working with young children should be sensitized to the need for immediate response to incidents of bullying, and that both teachers and children should be taught to recognize verbal intimidation and aggression as forms of bullying.

Since it is possible that students in some circumstances resort to bullying as an alternative to being in the role of victim, analysis of the school setting to ensure students' personal safety is necessary. Since it is also possible that students may resort to bullying in response to negative environmental models where aggressive behavior is reinforced, interventions should address development of social skills that will provide children with powerful positive techniques for controlling their environments.

In conclusion, future research should support the development of interventions that "immunize" young children from gang and violent behavior through preventative measures and early intervention when bullying occurs. Longitudinal examination of the effects of programs that target young children for comprehensive intervention in the forms of the development of safe schools and social skills is indicated. The results of the study also support the need for specific training of individuals working with young children in prevention and intervention with bullying behavior.

SUGGESTIONS FOR EDUCATORS
The following suggestions are provided to help the school staff combat the problem of bullying school-wide.

1. Educators should cooperatively plan to examine their school environment for signs of bullying. This examination may entail educators implementing direct observation of any place where two or more students gather, e.g. the hallways, the classroom, the lunchroom, the restrooms, the bus stop and the playground. Parents could assist in this task by observing their child's behavior at home, at the bus stop and in play. Bus drivers are also encouraged to contribute to the task with information about various behaviors observed on the school bus. The seeking and gathering of information about antisocial/bullying behaviors in various situations by school staff, parents and bus drivers should be shared and discussed in an open meeting, thus allowing persons to air their views about the problem and possible solutions.

2. Educators should take the time and talk to their students about bullying. They should also listen carefully to the concerns of their students about the problem and take notes on possible solutions. These informal discussions could be either with individuals (one on one), in small groups or with the entire class. Through student information, educators have the opportunity to gather knowledge about bullying from a different perspective - the student's view.

3. The use of anonymous student questionnaires is another way educators could gather information. Because some students are reluctant to speak out in front of others, the anonymous student questionnaire is a safe way for those students to be heard. The purpose at this point is to gather as much information as possible on the problem of bullying in the school.

4. Educators and staff members should plan and prepare for training on the problem of bullying, means that are available for identifying bullying behavior, and information on the various prevention and intervention programs for combating bullying behaviors. This training may consist of workshops, with outside help from professionals. The goal of the training session is to equip educators and staff members with the means to construct a school-wide anti-bullying program.

5. Educators and staff members should cooperatively establish school goals, policies and procedures for a safe learning environment. Educators and staff members should also establish and agree upon what consequences will be used school-wide for inappropriate behaviors. Consequences should be stated clearly and completely with one clear message - bullying behavior will not be tolerated in the school.

6. All students should be informed about the consequences of bullying behavior. A school assembly is one of the best ways to inform all students about any major school-wide concern. A school-wide assembly allows the students to see that all school members, e.g. teachers, staff, administrators, etc.. are all united on the cause.

Consequences may include:
1. informing parents of the behavior,
2. time-out,
3. loss of privileges,
4. detention, and/or in-school suspension.

Consequences should not be as negative as putting the student out of school. Rather, consequences should be designed to result in a positive outcome by keeping the student in school and teaching him/her acceptable behaviors.

Educators, staff members and parents should adopt an existing program or tailor make a program that would address their problems related to bullying. Note of caution: all schools may not experience problems with all of the bullying behaviors; therefore, it is wise to address those behaviors specific to each individual school.

Educators should be prepared to modify their ongoing activities to include anti-bullying messages, including teaching strategies, student training, immediate procedures in response to bullying behavior, preventative programs, and the larger curriculum.

Parents should be notified of the school's goals, policies, procedures and consequences related to inappropriate behaviors in school. The notification should explain why the school has established such goals, policies, procedures and consequences and encourage all parents to feel free to contribute information they may hear or know about concerning their child or any student being a bully or a victim. And most of all, the notification should stress the main goal - to establish a safe environment without fear, so that all students have the opportunity to learn.

Educators should take the initiative to involve all students in the procedures for "bully-proofing" their school. Students could contribute by making "Anti-Bullying" or "No Bullying Allowed" posters and displaying them throughout the school. Students could also create "No Bullying Allowed" buttons and wear them in school. These are only a few suggestions; students may create more.

SUGGESTIONS FOR THE CLASSROOM

1. Educators should discuss bullying behavior with their students. This discussion should include the nature of bullying, why some students bully others and the harm bullying can cause others. Educators should also discuss the meaning and consequences of harassment, teasing, racial putdowns and aggressive behaviors.

2. Educators should teach their students how to recognize a bully, if they are being bullies themselves, or if they are a victim. An excellent resource for this discussion or additional instruction is Garrity, et al., (1997) *Bully-Proofing Your School*. This book addresses bullying at all grade levels and gives clear explanations of bullying at the student's level of understanding. It also suggests topics for further discussion among the students.

3. Educators should establish clear classroom rules about bullying and the consequences for such activities. The rules can be a joint effort of the

entire class. The rules should contain what behaviors are not allowed in the classroom. Consequences for breaking the class rules should be spelled out, and both classroom rules and consequences should be posted so all students can see what is acceptable behavior and what is not. An excellent resource for this discussion is John, B., & Keeman, J.P. (1997), *Techniques for Managing a Safe School.*

4. Educators should teach students skills for resolving classroom conflicts non-violently. These skills will help the bully and the victim better understand the incident and what to do in a conflict-ridden situation. A resource for resolving classroom conflicts is Johnson & Johnson, (1995), *Reducing School Violence Through Conflict Resolution.*

5. Educators should teach students skills for acceptable ways to express their feelings, understand the feelings of others and acquire self-control techniques. Role-playing is an approach that could provide the opportunity for students to achieve such skills.

Role-playing appears to be a type of behavioral rehearsal which could be advantageous for the classroom setting, allowing students to practice dealing with various forms of unacceptable interactions including classroom conflicts, disruptive behaviors and bullying. With this approach, students can express their feelings and practice how to interact and resolve conflict in a positive manner. Bandura and Kupers (1964) stated that modeling was important for the development of self-control because various behaviors are often adopted from observed models. Role-playing could serve as a modeling function for self-control for other members of the class to observe.

Reverse role-playing is another way for students to understand the feelings of others. This activity will allow the students to present the other person's position and feelings by switching roles in their presentation. One main advantage of role-playing or reverse role-playing is that it encourages practicing positive interactions for specific situations.

6. Educators should teach students the skills for using bibliotherapy. This is a classroom teaching technique that uses reading materials to help students understand themselves and their problems. Through identification with the characters in the book or other reading materials, the student can achieve a better understanding of him/herself. Characteristics, attitudes, values and situations from the reading can serve as models for the student (Mercer & Mercer, 1993). Bibliotherapy activities encourage the students to retell their story with emphasis on incidents, feelings and behaviors. Students may also discuss changes they could have made as well as explore various consequences and alternative behaviors. Through bibliotherapy, students have the opportunity to learn that there is more than one way to solve a problem.

7. Educators should teach their students the skills needed for cooperative learning. In cooperative learning, students, both bullies and victims, can learn how to work together as a team to complete activities or assignments. According to Johnson, Johnson and Holubec (1993), cooperative learning is superior to both competitive learning and individualistic learning. For example, in competitive situations, students learn how to outdo each

other, which could develop into classroom conflict and poor socialization skills. In individualistic situations, students learn how to work alone, and their achievements are unrelated to those of other students. Because of the lack of interaction among students in an individualistic learning environment, positive socialization appears near zero.

On the other hand, cooperative learning increases the student's opportunity to experience success through sharing ideas and working together. It also provides students, especially bullies, the needed practice in school skills and positive social interaction by promoting step-by-step developments of social skills (Slavin, 1990). For many students, cooperative learning allows the student to develop appropriate social skills that can improve their chances of gaining social acceptance without aggressive behaviors.

CONCLUSION

Throughout this chapter, we have examined the various issues in the phenomenon of bullying behavior in school. And from this research, it appears that the schools are becoming a breeding ground for bullying behavior. To think that such a statement could be true is enough to motivate educators to think about what is being allowed in their schools. As educators, we should ask ourselves, "Are we condoning antisocial/aggressive behavior by ignoring it? Are we looking the other way when these aggressive behaviors take place because the students are young? Or, are we as educators allowing inappropriate behaviors to exist because we believe that it is just a part of growing up?" If yes is the answer to any of these questions, then as educators we are promoting bullying behavior. When such behaviors are not responded to or are ignored by educators or administrators, more serious events are likely to occur.

As educators, we cannot control all bullying behavior everywhere. But, as educators, we can learn how to control bullying behavior in the school and in our classrooms. If we, the educators, can control bullying behavior in the early stages of the child's development, we stand a better chance of stopping bullying behavior in the child's later stages of life. Then, as educators, we can get on with our business of "teaching" and providing all students with the opportunity to learn.

REFERENCES

Albanese, J.S. (1994). *Dealing with delinquency: The future of juvenile justice*. Chicago: Nelson-Hall Publishing.

Askew, A. (1998).   Aggressive behavior in boys. In D.P. and D.A. Lane (Eds.), *Bullying in schools* (pp. 4-7). Stoke-on-Trent: Trentham Books.

Bandura, A. (1973). *Aggression: A social learning analysis*. Englewood Cliffs, N.J.: Prentice Hall.

Bandura, A. and Kupers, C.J. (1964). Transmission of patterns of self-reinforcement through modeling. *Journal of Abnormal and Social Psychology, 69*(1).

Barr, R.D., and Parrett, W.H. (1995). *Hope at last for at-risk youth*. Boston: Allyn and Bacon.

Besag, V.E. (1989). *Bullies and victims in schools: A guide to understanding and management*. Milton Keynes, England: Open University Press.

Bowers, L., Smith, P.K., and Binney, V. (1994). Cohesion and power in the families of children involved in bully/victim problems at school." *Journal of Family Therapy*, 14, 371-387.

Bornfield, S. (1987). We will remember bullies 50 years from now. In National School Safety Center, *School bullying and victimization*. Malibu, CA: Pepperdine University Printing.

Bornfield, S., and Lantor, L. (1987). Bullies plague schools. *Gazette*. Chillicothe, OH: Gannett News Service.

Bjorqvist, K., Elman, K., and Largerspetz, K. (1982). Bullies and victims: Their ego picture and normative ego picture. *Scandanavian Journal of Psychology*, 23, 397-313.

Elkind, D., and Weiner, I.B. (1978). *Development of the child*. New York: Wiley.

Fox 5, Eyewitness News. (Dec. 10,1997). Teenager kills two students and wounds others -- Kentucky.

Garrity, C., Jens, K., Porter, W., Sager, N., and Shor-Camilli, C. (1997). *Bully-proofing your school: A comprehensive approach for elementary schools*. Longmont, CO: Sopris West.

Goldstein, A.P. and Conoley, J.C. (1997). *School violence intervention: A practical handbook*. New York: The Guilford Press.

Greenbaum, S., Garrison, R., James, B., and Stephens, R. (1989). School bullying and victimization. National School Safety Center. Malibu, CA: Pepperdine University.

Hawkins, J.D. (1996). *Delinquency and crime: Current theories*. Cambridge:University Press.

Hazler, R.J. (1994). Bullying breeds violence: You can stop it. *Learning*, February, 38-41.

Henineman, P.P. (1972). *Mobbing-gruppvald bland barnoch vuxna*. Stockholm: Natur ork Kultur.

Holmes, S.R. (1995). Views from the field: Potential research areas for addressing gang violence. *Journal of Gang Research*, 2(4), 53-57.

Holmes, S.R. (1997). Intervention in early stages of gang involvement. Presented at The First International Gang Specialist Training Program. Chicago, IL.

Holmes, S.R. (1997). Bullies. In George W. Knox, et al, *The facts about gang life in America today: A national study of over 4,000 gang members*. Chicago: National Gang Crime Research Center.

Holmes, S.R. and Brandenburg-Ayres, S.J. (1998). Bullying behavior in school: A predictor of later gang involvement. *Journal of Gang Research*, 5(2), 1-6.

Hoover, J.H., and Juul, K. (1993). Bullying in Europe and the United States. *Journal of Emotional and Behavioral Problems*, 2, 25-29.

Hoover, J.H. and Hazler, R.T. (1991). Bullies and victims. *Elementary School Guidance and Counseling*, 25, 212-219.

Hoover, J.H., Oliver, R.L., and Hazler, R.J. (1992). Bullying: Perception of adolescent victims in the midwestern U.S.A. *School Psychology International*, 13(1), 5-16.

Jensen, M.M., and Yerington, P.C. (1997). *Gangs: Straight talk, straight up*. Longmont, CO: Sopris West.

John, B.H., and Carr, V.G. (1995). *Technology for managing verbally and physically aggressive students*. Denver: Love Pub. Co.

Johnson, D.W., Johnson, R.T., and Holubec, E.J. (1993). *Cooperation in the classroom*. Edina, MI: Interaction Book Co.

Kelly, E, and Cohn, T. (1988) *Racism in school: New research evidence*. Stoke-on-Trent, London: Trentham Books.

Knox, G.W. (1994). *An introduction to gangs*. Bristol, IN: Wyndham Hall Press.

Knox, G.W., et al. (1997). *The facts about gang life in America today: A national study of over 4,000 gang members*. Chicago: The National Gang Crime Research Center.

Lane, D. (1989). Bullying in school: The need for an integrated approach. *School Psychology International*, 10, 211-215.

Maccoby, E.E. (1986). Social grouping in childhood: Their relationships to prosocial and antisocial behavior in boys and girls. In D. Olewus, J. Block, and M. Radke-Yarrow (Eds.), *Development of antisocial and prosocial behavior*. New York: Academia Press.

Maccoby, E.E. and Jacklin, C.N. (1980). Sex differences in aggression: A rejoinder and reprise. *Child Development*, 51, 964-80.

Malik, G. (1990). *Bullying - An investigation of race and gender aspects*. Unpublsihed MSc Thesis, University of Sheffield.

Maloney, M. (1995). How dangerous are our schools? *School Violence Alert*, 1 (1), 6-7.

Manning, M.L. and Raruth, L.G. (1995). *Students at risk*. Boston: Allyn and Bacon.

Mercer, C.D. and Mercer, A.R. (1993). *Teaching students with learning problems*. New York: Macmillan Publising Company.

Mooney, A., Creeser, R., and Blatchford, P. (1991). Children's views on teasing and fighting in junior schools. *Educational Research*, 33(2), 103-112.

Munthe, E. (1989). Bullying in Scandanavia. In E. Munthe and E. Roland (Eds.), *Bullying: An international perspective* (pp. 66-78). London: Professional Development Foundation.

Newson, E. and Newson, J. (1984). Parents perspective on children's behavior at school. In N. Frudem and H. Gault (Eds.), *Disruptive behavior in schools*. New York: Wiley.

Olweus, D. (1984). Aggressors and their victims: bullying at school. In N. Frude and H. Gault (Eds.), *Disruptive behavior in schools*. New York: Wiley.

Olweus, D. (1987). *Aggression in the schools: Bullies and whipping boys*. New York: Wiley.

Olweus, D. (1993). *Bullying at school: What we know and what we can do*. Cambridge: Blackwell.

Olweus, D. (1994). Bullying: Too little love, too much freedom. *School Safety*. National School Safety Center, News Service. Malibu, CA: Pepperdine University Press.

Osofsky, J.D. (Ed.), (1997). *Children in a violent society*. New York: The Guilford Press.

Perry, D.G., Kusel, S.J., and Perry, L.C. (1988). Victims of peer aggression. *Development Psychology*, 24(6), 807-814.

Pulkkinen, L, and Tremblelay, R.E. (1992). Patterns of boy's social adjustment in two cultures and at different ages: A longitudinal perspective. *International Journal of Behavioral Development*, 15, 527-53.

Roland, E. (1988). Bullying: The Scandanavian research tradition. In D.P. Tattum and D.A. Lane (Eds.), *Bullying in Schools*. Stoke-on-Trent: Trentham Books.

Rutherford, R.B. and Nelson, C.M. (1995). Management of aggressive and violent behavior in schools. *Focus on Exceptional Children*, 27(6), 1-16.

School safety update. (1994). National School Safety Center, News Center. Westlake Village, CA: Pepperdine University Press.

Shanker, A. (1995). Classroom Held Hostage. *American Educator*, 19(1), 8-13.

Shelly, L.I. (1995). American crime: An international anomaly? *Comparative Social Research*, 8, 81-85.

Slavin, R.E. (1990). *Cooperative learning: Theory, research, and practice*. Englewood Cliffs, NJ: Prentice Hall.

Slee, P.T. (1993). Bullying: A preliminary investigation of its nature and effects of social cognition. *Early Child Development and Care*, 87, 47-57.

Smith, P.K. (1991). The silent nightmare: Bullying and victimization in school peer groups. *The Psychologists Bulletin of the British Psychological Society*, 4, 243-248.

Snyder, H. N. (1997). Juvenile arrests 1996. *Juvenile Justice Bulletin*, Nov. Washington, D.C.: U.S. Department of Justice, Office of Justice Programs, Office of Juvenile Justice and Delinquency Prevention.

Stephenson, P. and Smith, D. (1989). Bullying in the junior school. In D.P. Tattum and D.A. Lane (Eds.), *Bullying in Schools*. Stoke-on-Trent: Trentham Books.

Stepp, L.S. (1992). Getting tough with big, bad, bullies: Girls are not exempt. *The Washington Post*, December 1.

Troy, M, and Scoufe, L.A. (1987). Victimization among preschoolers: Role of attachment relationship history. *Journal of the American Academy of Child and Adolescent Psychiatry*, 26, 166-172.

Webster, D.T. (1991). *Why is everybody always picking on me? A guide to Understanding bullies*. Middlebury, CT: Atrium Society.

Whelan, R.J. (1998). *Emotional and behavioral disorders*. Denver, CO: Love Publishing Company.

Whitney, I., and Smith, P.K. (1993). A survey of the nature and extent of bullying in junior/middle and secondary schools. *Educational Research*, 35, 2-25.

Wilson, J.Q., and Petesilia, J. (1995). *Crime*. San Francisco, CA: Institute for Contemporary Studies Press.

CHAPTER FOUR

FAMILY DYNAMICS:
GANG MEMBERS VS. NON-GANG MEMBERS

Jodet-Marie Harris, Ed.D.
Jackson State University

Criminologists have long recognized the importance of family in the prevention of delinquency (Knox, 1991; Knox, Laske, & Tromanhauser, 1993) as well as in the etiology of delinquency (Taylor, 1990; Jankowski, 1991). According to Knox (1991), parents are the first line of defense against the gang problem. In a survey designed to get the perspectives of parents, police officers, principals and school volunteers of what can be done about the gang problem, the consensus was that the family can prevent gang affiliation (Knox, Laske, & Tromanhauser, 1993). The National School Safety study, Gangs in Schools, noted that "with a little knowledge and understanding of the gang phenomenon, adults may help stem the tide of gang affiliation and its natural accompaniments: disrespect, disruption in school and the vicious cycle of community violence" (p. 2). Another study noted that one-third of the gang members reported that their parents did not know they were with a gang, and an equal percentage responded that their parents knew of their affiliation and did not like it (Schwartz, 1989). Moore (1990) reported that a surprisingly large proportion of gang members, even in notorious gangs, were able to hide their membership from their parents who are working, preoccupied with a large family or believe their child is playing with one of the numerous adolescent groups in the neighborhood.

Additional research on the family's connection to delinquency examined the relationship between the "broken family" and delinquency (Farnsworth, 1984; Matsueda & Heimer, 1987; Moynihan, 1965; Rankin, 1983). Rosen (1968) noted that delinquents were more likely to come from families that had a deviant structure, deviant family relationships, or passed on deviant norms to their offspring. These findings were confirmed later by a number of researchers. Marquis (1992) studied 118 inmates and 45 college students in Canada to investigate if chaotic family history is a risk factor for later antisocial behavior. Chaotic family history was operationalized as parental breakup, parental alcoholism, physical abuse, sexual abuse, foster care placement, or being adopted. The results confirmed that turbulent family history is a risk factor for later delinquency. In his study of Detroit gangs, Taylor (1989) reported on a single mother that approved of her children's involvement in gangs because it provided them with status in the community and financial independence. Similarly, Jankowski (1991) noted that in a number of areas parents have encouraged their own children to be active in gangs, and some have encouraged other people's children to do so. Additionally, he noted that 32% of the fathers interviewed in the Los Angles area had been in the same gang as their children, and about 11% said that four generations of men in their family had been in the same gang.

Other studies have examined the connection between poor parental supervision and delinquency. Glueck & Glueck (1970) investigated 500 delinquent and 500 non-delinquent boys from the Boston area. They discovered that maternal supervision was one of the factors that distinguished delinquents from non-delinquents. Jensen (1972) found a significant negative relationship between parental supervision and self-reported delinquency. Gang members' quality of family interaction, supervision and discipline, family affection patterns, and maternal attitudes toward males differ between gang and non-gang members (Synder, 1990). The purpose of this investigation was to examine the differences between the family dynamics of gang members versus non-gang members and to increase our understanding of the role, if any, the family plays in the behavior of gang members.

METHODOLOGY

Data used for this analysis came from Project GANGFACT, a self-report survey completed by approximately 10,000 juveniles and young adults in a variety of correctional facilities and programs across the country. About 4,000 of the respondents were self-proclaimed gang members. A detailed description of the methodology of the study can be found in Chapter Two.

Several of the co-principal investigators of Project GANGFACT developed hypotheses involving aspects of family life. These hypotheses provided the basis for several items included on the survey designed to capture critical elements of family structure, family dynamics, and overall quality of family life. These hypotheses were used to develop an index of family dysfunction for self-reported gang members (N = 4,140) and non-gang members (N = 5,585). The additive index of family dysfunction was created from the

following 10 different family factors:
- non-intact family structure;
- parental knowledge of gang membership;
- father encouraged the child to join a gang;
- mother encouraged the child to join a gang;
- parents would be embarrassed to learn their child was a gang member;
- parents who show favorable attitudes toward drugs, crime, and violence;
- a parent who served time in prison;
- parents who did not take the time to come and meet with teachers when the youth was in school;
- parents who were physically violent in the home; and
- lack of parental support.

An arbitrary value of "1" was assigned for responses to the items that were measures of different aspects of family dysfunction. Thus, with 10 different factors, the range of possible scores on the family dysfunction scale varied between an absolute low score of "zero" (where we would assume family cohesion) to an absolute high of "ten" (where we would assume a high level of family dysfunction).

Description of Family Factors

Non-intact family structure was measured by asking, "which statement best describes your Family?" ___mother, father, and siblings ___mother, myself, and siblings ___father, myself, and siblings. Any respondent that reported a family structure other than mother, father, and siblings gained one point on the family dysfunction scale for a non-intact family structure.

Parental knowledge of gang membership was measured by the item, "do your parents know you are a member of a gang?" A response of "yes" earned respondents a point on the family dysfunction scale because it was assumed that respondents were not being sanctioned by their parents for gang affiliation.

Father encouraged child to join a gang was measured by a true/false question: "my father encouraged me to join a gang." A response of "true" earned one point on the family dysfunction scale.

Mother encouraged child to join a gang was measured by a true/false question: "my mother encouraged me to join a gang." A response of "true" earned one point on the family dysfunction scale.

Parent would be embarrassed to learn their child was a gang member was measured by a true/false question: "my mother and father would be embarrassed if they knew I was in a gang." A response of "false" to this item earned the respondent one point on the family dysfunction scale.

Parents showed positive attitudes toward drugs, crime, and violence was measured by the question, "my parent(s) often show favorable attitudes toward drugs, crime, and violence." Responses were based on a continuum from strongly agree to strongly disagree. Responses of strongly agree or agree earned one point on the family dysfunction scale.

Whether the respondent had a parent who had served time in prison was measured by asking, "have either of your parents ever served time in prison?" A response of "yes" earned one point for the respondent on the family dysfunction scale.

Whether parents took the time to come and meet with teachers when the youth was in school was measured by the item, "my parent(s) took time to come and meet my teachers when I was in school." Responses were based on a continuum of always to never. An answer of "rarely" or "never" earned the respondent one point on the family dysfunction scale.

Whether parents were physically violent in the home was measured by the item, "my parent(s) were physically violent in my home." Responses were based on a continuum from always to never. Responses of "always "or "usually" earned the respondent a point on the family dysfunction scale.

Lack of parental supervision was measured by asking, "my parent(s) knew where I was and who I was with." Responses were based on a continuum from always to never. Responses of "never" or "rarely" earned the respondent one point on the family dysfunction scale.

RESULTS

TABLE 1
FREQUENCY AND PERCENTAGE DISTRIBUTION OF FAMILY DYSFUNCTION SCALE SCORES FOR GANG MEMBERS VERSUS NON-GANG MEMBERS

Family Dysfunction Scores	Non-Gang Members		Gang Members	
	Number	Percent	Number	Percent
0	1736	31.1	286	6.9
1	2254	40.3	800	19.3
2	1034	18.5	975	23.6
3	381	6.8	976	23.6
4	126	2.3	630	15.2
5	40	0.7	276	6.7
6	11	0.2	126	3.0
7	2	0.04	48	1.2
8	1	0.02	15	0.4
9	0	0.0	6	0.1
10	0	0.0	2	0.02

The frequencies of the family dysfunction scale scores for gang members versus non-gang members are displayed in Table 1. As expected, non-gang members were more likely to have resided in households with a lower level of family dysfunction than gang members. When examining individual family dysfunction items, the patterns were similar for the items applicable to both gang and non-gang members. Non-gang members were more likely than gang members to come from two-parent families (41.7% vs. 34.5%, Chi-square=49.1, p<.001). Gang members were more likely than non-gang members to have parents who showed favorable attitudes toward drugs, crime, and violence (22.4% vs. 17.4%, Chi-square=17.4, p=.002). Gang members were more likely than non-gang members to report that their parent(s) had served time in prison (39.8% vs. 22.1%, Chi-square=285.4, p<.001). Gang members were somewhat more likely to come from a physically violent household than non-gang members, but this difference was not great (15.1% vs. 12.2%, Chi-square=15.1, p=.004). Gang members were less likely than non-gang members to have parental supervision, as indicated by the responses "rarely" or "never" (36.0% vs. 22.8%, Chi-square=198.6, p<.001). There was not a remarkable difference, however, between gang members and non-gang members in terms of the level of their parents' involvement in their education, with about half being "always" or "usually" involved (52.2%), and the rest being involved "sometimes" (25.5%), "rarely" (10.5%), or "never" (11.9%). Clearly, gang members' family backgrounds have higher levels of dysfunction than non-gang members, as reflected by this scale.

TABLE 2

GANG MEMBERSHIP BY FAMILY DYSFUNCTION SCORE

| | Family Dysfunction Score | | | | |
| | Low Dysfunction | | High Dysfunction | | |
	Number	%	Number	%	Total
Gang Member:					
NO	5024	89.9	561	10.1	5585
YES	2061	49.8	2079	50.2	4140
Total	7085	72.9	2640	27.2	9725

Chi Square = 1940.126, p = .000, Gamma = .80

Table 2 divides the sample of gang members and non-gang members into two groups based on family dysfunction scale scores. Persons with a scale score of 2 or under accounted for 89.9% of the sample of non-gang members and 49.8% of the sample of gang members. Those with a family dysfunction scale score of 3 or higher accounted for 50.2% of the sample of gang members and 10.1% of the sample of non-gang members. The association between gang membership and high family dysfunction was statistically significant (Chi-square=1940.126, p=.000), and measure of association (Gamma) was high (.80) in the predicted direction. In other words, the data support that gang members have a significantly more dysfunctional family background compared to non-gang members.

SUMMARY AND CONCLUSIONS
Overall, as hypothesized, the results of this study support previous findings that indicate that gang members are more likely to come from highly dysfunctional families. In this particular study, family dysfunction was measured by the creation of a scale derived from 10 items on the survey, and respondents with three or more family dysfunction factors were considered to be from highly dysfunctional families. In regard to considering parents as a first line of defense against gang involvement, the data reported here indicate that gang members were more likely to come from families that supported or encouraged their gang involvement. Thus these results suggest that parental education programs must play a large part in the prevention of gang involvement.
Further research regarding which family dysfunction variables are the greatest predictors of gang involvement need to be conducted. However, given what we already know, proactive policies and programs designed to strengthen families need to be developed to prevent children from becoming involved in gangs.

REFERENCES
Farnsworth, M. 1984. Family structure, family attributes and delinquency in a sample of low-income, minority males and females. *Journal of Youth and Adolescence*, 13(4), pp. 349-364.

Glueck, F. and Glueck, E. 1970. *Toward a typology of juvenile offenders*. New York: Grune and Stratton.

Jensen, G. F. and Rojek, D. G. 1980. Contexts for adolescent socialization. In *Delinquency: A sociological view*, pp. 192-225.

Knox, G. W. 1991. *Introduction to gangs*. Berrien Springs, MI: Vande Vere Publishing Ltd.

Knox, G. W., Laske, D. L., and Tromanhauser, E. D. 1992. *Schools under siege*. Dubuque, Iowa: Kendall/Hunt Publishing, Company.

Jankowski, M. S. 1991. *Islands in the street: Gangs and American urban society*. Berkeley, CA: University of California Press.

Marquis, P. 1992. Family dysfunction as a risk factor in the development of antisocial behavior. *Psychological Reports*, 71, pp. 468-470.

Matsueda, R. L. & Heimer, K. 1983. Race, family structure, and delinquency: A test of differential association and social control theories. *American Sociological Review*, 52, pp. 826-840.

Moore, J.   1990.   Gangs, drugs, violence.   In M. De la Rosa, E. Y. Lambert, & B. Gropper, (Eds.), NIDA Research Monograph, 103, pp. 160-176.   Washington, D.C.: United States Department of Health & Human Services, Public Health Services, Alcohol, Drug Abuse and Mental Health Administration, National Institute on Drug Abuse.

Moynihan, D.   1965.   *The negro family: A case of naitonal action*.   Washington, D.C.: United States Department of Labor.

National School Safety Study.   1991.   *Gangs in schools: Breaking up is hard to do*.   Malibu, CA: Pepperdine University.

Rankin, J. H.   1983.   The family context in deliquency.   *Social Problems*, 30(4), pp. 466-479.

Rosen, L.   1969.   Broken homes.   In L. Savitz & N. Johnston (Eds.), *Comtemporary Criminology*.   New York: John Wiley & Sons.

Taylor, C.   1990.   *Dangerous society*.   East Lansing, MI: Michigan State University Press.

CHAPTER FIVE

RISK FACTORS ASSOCIATED WITH GANG JOINING AMONG YOUTH

Sandra S. Stone, Ph.D.
State University of West Georgia

Why do children join gangs? This question has plagued successive generations of parents, teachers, public safety officials, community leaders and policy makers for well over a century. Numerous theories have been proposed regarding psychological and sociological conditions that give rise to gang formation. Beginning in the 1920s, researchers at the University of Chicago discussed gang formation as a result of social disorganization in certain neighborhoods where gangs provide a source of structure and informal social control missing from families and other social institutions (Shaw and McKay, 1942). Later, Merton (1938) suggested that criminal and delinquent behavior result from the strain experienced when legitimate opportunities are not available to support the attainment of mainstream social goals. Cohen (1955) used the assumptions of Merton's strain theory to develop his theory of delinquent subcultures (i.e. gangs), positing that children who are unable to adequately meet middle-class standards and achieve legitimate success suffer status frustration. Consequently, they join together in gangs and behave in ways that are "nonutilitarian, malicious, and negativistic." Miller (1958) also proposed the existence of a lower-class subculture that gives rise to delinquent gangs.

Sutherland (1939) theorized that criminal and delinquent behaviors emerge through a learning process that occurs in intimate social groups that favor and reinforce such activities over more law-abiding behaviors. Thus, individuals learn to engage in delinquent behavior through association with delinquent peer groups, including gangs, which socialize them into a life of crime through modeling, providing favorable definitions of illegal behavior, and reinforcing illegal acts. Further, Hirschi (1969) maintained that criminal and delinquent behaviors arise from weakened ties to conventional society. The social bond an individual maintains with society includes attachment to significant others (especially family), commitment to conventional goals and means to reach them, involvement in conventional activities, and sharing common moral beliefs of mainstream society. As one or more of these elements of the social bond become weakened, the individual becomes more likely to engage in delinquent behavior, including association with gangs.

While these theories, which have had mixed reviews in terms of empirical support, address the psycho-social conditions that may give rise to and help maintain gangs, they do not really address the motivations for individual children to join a particular gang. Studies of Puerto-Rican (Padillo, 1992) and Chicano (Vigil, 1988) gangs suggest that in some neighborhoods where gangs have been a main fixture for decades, youths are socialized into the gang beginning at an early age and do not so much decide to join as they do to declare their membership as more official. On the other hand, Jankowski (1990) describes a more formal process of joining a gang, where a deliberate decision is made to join, and the gang agrees to accept the person as a member. According to his typology, there are six main reasons for joining a gang: monetary gain, recreation, refuge, protection, resistance to becoming like their parents, and commitment to community. Individuals may join gangs for one or more of the identified reasons, but the decision is a deliberate one which the individual believes is in his/her own best interest. Other reasons cited for joining gangs include companionship, excitement, acceptance, a sense of identity, status, success, respect and a sense of belonging (Hochhaus and Sousa, 1988; Reiner, 1992). In addition, professionals who work with delinquent youths, and even the youths themselves, often say that gangs become surrogate families for their members, providing the structure and care missing for these youths at home. And, youths may join gangs because they do not have anything else to do.

Another approach has been to examine a constellation of dysfunctional behaviors most likely initiated in adolescence (i.e. delinquency, violence, drug use, teen pregnancy, dropping out of school, gang involvement) and determine those factors in an individual's life that increase the likelihood these behaviors will occur. Work in the area of prevention led Hawkins and Catalano (1993) to identify several risk factors in different domains of a child/adolescent's life that significantly contributed to the likelihood that he/she would become involved in delinquency, violence and/or drug use, all activities associated with gangs (See Table 1).

TABLE 1

RISK FACTORS FOR ENGAGING IN DELINQUENCY, DRUGS AND VIOLENCE

Individual/Peer

Rebelliousness
Have friends who engage in the problem behavior
Have favorable attitudes toward the problem behavior
Early initiation of the problem behavior
Constitutional factors (e.g. Attention Deficit Hyperactive
Disorder, Anti-Social Personality Disorder, biological factors)

Family

Family history of the problem behavior
Family management problems
Family conflict, including partner and/or child abuse
Favorable parental attitudes/involvement in problem behavior

School

Early and persistent antisocial behavior
Academic failure beginning in elementary school
Lack of commitment to school

Community

Availability of drugs
Availability of firearms
Community laws and norms favorable toward drugs, guns and crime
Media portrayals of violence
Transitions and mobility
Low neighborhood attachment and community disorganization
Extreme economic deprivation

Source: Hawkins and Catalano (1993)

Similarly, Spergel and Curry (1992) identified causal factors leading to gang involvement among youth (see Table 2).

TABLE 2

FACTORS LEADING TO GANG INVOLVEMENT AMONG YOUTH

Individual Problems

Drug and alcohol use
Peer and gang influences
Self-protection and fear of gangs
Lack of self-esteem and other psychological explanations

Institutional Failures

Family breakdown
School failure/"dropouts"
Lack of role models

Structural Causes

Poverty
Unemployment
Criminal opportunity
Increase in availability and profit of drug sales
Changes in population

Response Effects

Failure of the legal system
Lack of community services
Media
Discrimination
Denial
Labeling

Source: Spergel and Curry (1992)

In an effort to better understand all facets of gang involvement, including why youths join gangs, the National Gang Crime Research Center recently conducted the largest survey of gang members to date. During the spring and summer of 1996, a collaborative effort of 28 researchers in 17 different states surveyed about 10,000 youths and adults in a variety of correctional settings. Approximately 4,000 of the respondents reported that they had been a member of a gang at some point, and close to two-thirds of those indicated that they were active members at the time of the survey. The rest of the chapter will explain Project GANGFACT, discuss the methodology, then focus on those items specifically relating to gang joining behavior.

One of the hypotheses being tested in this study about gang joining behavior is that if more positive alternatives were available to youths, they would be less inclined to join a gang. Three areas were specifically explored -- money, protection and recreation. The hypotheses are that if they had other opportunities to make money, if they felt safe at home and in their communities, and if other social and/or recreational activities were available, the gang culture would not be as appealing. This paper will also examine whether the data from this survey substantiate the work of Hawkins and Catalano (1993) and Spergel and Curry (1992) as it relates to multiple problem areas that give rise to delinquent behavior, including involvement with gangs. More specifically, if the multi-problem perspective holds, for those youths who joined a gang in search of money, protection and recreation, risk factors associated with their decision to join a gang are likely to incorporate individual, family, school and community components. Further, the analyses for each of the three main reasons to join a gang being explored in this paper will be broken down by gender to determine whether risk factors may vary for males and females.

Background and Methodology of Project GANGFACT

Project GANGFACT is an acronym for Project **Gang Field Assessment of Crime Threat**. It seeks to clarify the facts about gang life in the United States today. The project was organized in 1995 by the National Gang Crime Research Center, and data for the project were gathered during 1996.

Project GANGFACT used the individual as the unit of analysis, and the research strategy was the anonymous "self-report" methodology frequently used in survey research. The idea was to collect new primary data directly from gang members. In an attempt to maximize the sample size, Project GANGFACT targeted the confined offender population (primarily juveniles) in 17 states and secured the collaboration of 28 researchers. The total number of individuals surveyed was 10,166, with a sample size of 4,140 self-reported gang members. These figures make the survey the single largest study of its kind ever undertaken and reported in the literature.

One of the goals of the Project GANGFACT research task force was to ensure that gang members were studied in a variety of social contexts. The types of programs/facilities used in the Project GANGFACT task force research, therefore, consisted of the following:
(1) Jails;
(2) Adult prisons;
(3) Boot camps;
(4) Local juvenile detention centers;
(5) Long term juvenile correctional institutions; and
(6) Private residential facilities and private correctional;

facilities, DUI and Work Release centers, etc.

Completed surveys were sent to the National Gang Crime Research Center in Chicago for data entry and analysis.

For additional information on Project GANGFACT and the methodology of the study, please see Chapter Two of this monograph and/or contact The National Gang Crime Research Center to request a copy of the full report.

SAMPLING OVER 4,000 GANG MEMBERS

Gang research that samples only from one city or one state has historically been a source of contradictory and confusing research results in the gang research arena. One goal of the study was to have representative national data, so the research covered multiple states and both large and small jurisdictions. Please see Figure 1 at the end of Chapter Two and/or the full report available from NGCRC for a complete listing of the 75 sites with the total number of respondents from each site as well as the number who were self-reported gang members.

In all settings, a saturation sampling technique was sought. This meant everyone in the program/facility was asked to participate in the research. Sometimes incentives were used, and this resulted in upwards of 90 percent of the populations in these settings cooperating. Because of mixed populations in some of the facilities, our sample of gang members includes both juveniles and adults.

Internal Controls on Data Quality, Validity and Reliability

For a full discussion of internal controls on data quality, and reliability and validity of the survey instrument, please see Chapter Two of this monograph and/or the full report available from NGCRC. In brief, data quality was ensured through the following measures: both covert and overt observation of respondents completing the survey; zero tolerance for data entry or transcription errors; the fact that there were few unusable survey instruments; the establishment of an acceptable level of trust in each site; the indication that there was high cognition on the meaning of the survey items by respondents; and the fact that the survey contained built-in "lie detectors." In the opinion of the researchers, adequate precautions were taken to ensure that the survey was both valid and reliable.

RESULTS
Description of the Sample

The respondent population will be described, then the results will focus on three items specific to gang joining behavior -- the importance of making money, the importance of protection, and lack of other alternative activities.

Because some adults were included in the study in some of the sites, the age range for respondents was between 9 and 73. Precisely half (50%) were under 18, however, and about two-thirds (73%) were 25 or younger.

The mean age for the overall sample was 22 years, while the mean age for the gang member sub-sample was 19.

The gender distribution of the respondents closely resembles the gender distribution of the confined offender population in general. Approximately 89% of respondents were male, and 11% were females. The difference in gang membership between males and females was significant (chi square = 86.0, 1df, p <.001), with 44% of the males being gang members, compared to 30% of the females.

Approximately 30% of the sample was white, 52% was African-American, 10% was Hispanic, 1% was Asian, 3% was Native American Indian, 1% was Arab-American, and 4% was "other" (percentages exceed 100 due to rounding). The differences between racial/ethnic groups in terms of gang membership were significant (chi square =394.4, 6df, p <.001), with the following percentages of each group claiming to be in a gang: 42% African-Americans, 32% whites, 66% Hispanics, 67% Asians, 45% Native American Indians, 44% Arab-Americans, and 52% other.

In terms of family structure, 39% report having an intact, two-parent family, 53% report living in mother-headed households, and 9% report living in households headed by their father. There was a significant difference in family structure between gang members and non-gang members (chi square = 49.1, 2df, p < .001), with 42% of the non-gang members coming from two-parent families compared with 35% of the gang members.

One item on the survey attempted to measure the respondent's perception of his/her social class by asking, true or false, "I feel that I am not part of legitimate opportunities in my city or town and am cut out of good possibilities." Generally, 56% answered "false," and 44% answered "true." The difference between gang members and non-gang members was significant (chi square = 41.5, 1df, p < .001), with 41% of non-gang members feeling left out of legitimate opportunities and 48% of gang members feeling that way.

Respondents were also asked whether they had completed high school or the GED, and 65% indicated they had completed neither, while 35% had completed one or the other. This item, too, was significant when comparisons of gang members and non-gang members were made. Some 42% of non-gang members had obtained either a high school diploma or a GED, compared to only 25% of gang members (chi square = 304.1, 1df, p < .001).

So, generally, it seems that gang members are more likely to be young, minority males from female-headed households, who have not completed high school or obtained a GED and who perceive themselves to be closed off from legitimate opportunities.

Decisions to Join a Gang

The survey asked the question, "have you ever joined a gang?" In this national sample of offenders, 57% (N = 5585) indicated they had never joined a gang, but 43% (N = 4140) said they had. Those who had joined a gang constitute the sample that will be analyzed next.

In terms of age at which the respondent joined a gang, 87% had joined before their 16th birthday, and 98% had joined by the age of 18. Approximately three-fourths (78%) had joined on or before the age of 14, and close to half (45%) had joined on or before the age of 12. The mean age at time of first joining a gang was 12.7 years of age for this national sample. Approximately 8% (325) of those who claimed gang membership were female.

The survey asked the respondents whether they were affiliated with Crips, Bloods, People/Brothers, Folks, Surenos, Nortenos, or other. Some 23% indicated Crips, 9% Bloods, 12% People/Brothers, 26% Folks, 8% Surenos, 2% Nortenos, and some 20% "other," which contains groups such as skinheads, Aryan Brotherhood and motorcycle gangs.

The survey asked, "are you currently a member of any gang?" The responses showed that 65% (N = 2627) were still active in their gang, while some 35% (N = 1412) indicated they were no longer active.

The Importance of Making Money in the Decision to Join the Gang

The survey asked "how important was the chance to make money in your decision to join a gang", where the response modes included: very important, important, and not important. Approximately one-fourth (25%, N = 998) of the respondents indicated making money was "very important" in their decision to join a gang, and 29% (N = 1143) reported that making money was "important." Still, 46% (N = 1806) reported that making money was "not important" in their decision to join a gang. There was no significant difference between males and females.

Females

Table 3 lists the items that were significantly associated (< .05) with females for whom money was important in their decision to join a gang. Generally, these females think it is okay to demand that their needs be met, and they are likely to get what they want even if they have to take it; however, they tend to avoid activities that could lead to personal injury. They have more close friends in the gang than females for whom money was not an important factor, and their parents tend to show favorable attitudes towards drugs, crime and violence. They are more likely to say that their schools do not take drugs, guns and gangs seriously and that gang fighting is considered normal behavior in their neighborhoods.

TABLE 3
ITEMS SIGNIFICANTLY ASSOCIATED WITH FEMALES FOR WHOM MONEY
WAS IMPORTANT IN THEIR DECISION TO JOIN A GANG

ITEM	CHI-SQUARE	DF	SIGN
INDIVIDUAL/PEER			
Get what they want even if they have to take it	18.870	8	.016
Tend to be careful to avoid activities that could lead to injury	27.739	8	.001
Think it's ok to demand that their needs be met	21.654	8	.006
Some close friends in the gang	23.527	10	.009
FAMILY			
Parents show favorable attitudes towards drugs, crime and violence	33.595	8	.000
SCHOOL			
School doesn't take drugs, guns and gangs seriously	20.892	8	.007
COMMUNITY			
Gang fights are normal in n'hood	25.938	8	.001

Males

Those items significantly associated (p < .05) with males for whom money was important in their decision to join the gang are displayed in Table 4. The males for whom money was important are likely to be from a racial/ ethnic group other than Hispanic, their gang is more likely to be comprised of only one racial group, and they are likely to have many close friends in the gang. They tend to get what they want, even if they have to take it, and they believe it is okay to demand that their needs be met. As might be expected, they are more likely to have bullied others in school, and they tend to think that bullying may lead to gangbanging. These males tend to engage in risky behaviors that could lead to personal injury (e.g. selling crack), and they are more likely than those males for whom money was not important to report having been forced to have sex they did not want to have. They are less likely to attend church and more likely to say not only that they do not believe in God, but that they are on Satan's side.

Males for whom money was important in their decision to join the gang are more likely to have parents who know they are in the gang and who encouraged them to join. They are also more likely to have parents who show favorable attitudes towards drugs, crime and violence. Further, according to these males, their school does not take drugs, guns and gangs seriously.

Males who said money was an important reason for joining the gang are more likely to feel they are not a part of the legitimate opportunity structure and are shut out of good possibilities in life. They also do not believe they will be able to find a good job and support a family. They say gang fighting is normal behavior in their neighborhoods, and they are more likely to say they know law enforcement officials who are gang members.

TABLE 4

ITEMS SIGNIFICANTLY ASSOCIATED WITH MALES FOR WHOM MONEY WAS IMPORTANT IN THEIR DECISION TO JOIN A GANG

ITEM	CHI-SQUARE	DF	SIGN
INDIVIDUAL/PEER			
Do not believe they will be able to find a good job and support a family	15.979	2	.000
Get what they want even if they have to take it	143.818	8	.000
Bullied others in school	30.296	2	.000
Think bullying can lead to gangbanging	21.021	2	.000
Racial/ethnic group other than Hispanic	34.261	12	.001
Less likely to attend church	6.826	2	.000
Likely to engage in activities where they might be injured	42.474	8	.000
Believe it's ok to demand their needs be met	77.862	8	.000
Forced to have unwanted sex	9.791	2	.007
Do not believe in God	8.873	2	.012
Say they are on Satan's side	7.448	2	.024
Many close friends in the gang	108.516	10	.000
Gang mostly 1 racial group	17.662	4	.001

Table 4: Coninued

Family

Parents know about gang membership	12.434	2	.002
Father encouraged to join the gang	36.987	2	.000
Mother encouraged to join the gang	22.563	2	.000
Parents show favorable attitudes toward drugs, crime, and violence	52.651	8	.000

School

School does not take drugs, guns and gangs too seriously	39.482	8	.000

Community

Do not feel a part of legitimate opportunities	17.253	2	.000
Gang fighting is normal in n'hood	162.134	8	.000
Know law enforcement officials who are gang members	28.690	2	.000

SUMMARY

These results indicate that there are some similarities between males and females for whom making money was important in their decision to join a gang. Both think it is okay to demand that their needs be met, and they are likely to get what they want even if they have to take it. Both males and females have close friends in the gang and parents with favorable attitudes towards drugs, crime and violence. Both report lax attitudes about drugs, guns and gangs by their schools and say that gang fighting is normal in their neighborhoods.

Along with the similarities, there are also differences. Males are more likely to have been bullies in school, to have been sexually abused, and to engage in risky behaviors that put them at risk for personal injury. Males are more likely to believe they will not be able to find a good job and support a family, and they perceive that they lack legitimate opportunities to make money through legal means.

Thus, the notion that there may be gender differences holds true to some extent if money was an important factor in the decision to join the gang. It is also true that risk factors span all areas of the youths' lives for both males and females. And, the hypothesis that the availability of positive alternatives will decrease the likelihood of gang involvement may hold true if there are realistic alternatives for making money for males, but it may not hold true for alternatives that meet other social/emotional needs, as both males and females appear to be getting many of their social/emotional needs met by their involvement in the gang.

The Importance of Protection in the Decision to Join the Gang

The survey asked "how important was seeking protection in your decision to join a gang," where the response modes included: very important, important, and not important. Some 16% (N = 647) indicated that protection was very important, and some 25% (N = 973) reported that protection was important in their decision to join a gang. But, some 59% (N = 2354) reported that protection was not important in their decision to join a gang. There was a significant difference between males and females on this variable, with protection being more important for females than males (chi-square = 61.5, 2df, p < .001).

Females

Results for females for whom protection was important in their decision to join a gang can be found in Table 5. They report being more likely to have been bullied in school and more likely to have been forced to have sex. On the other hand, other significant items were that they were more likely to have bullied others and more likely to think that it is okay to demand that their needs be met. While these findings might appear to be contradictory, it may be that there are two types of females who join gangs for protection -- those who have been victimized and are truly seeking protection and those who are aggressors and are seeking group support for their activities, or protection in numbers.

Females who joined the gang for protection were likely to have parents who showed favorable attitudes towards drugs, crime and violence and to have mothers who encouraged them to join the gang. They are more likely to think their school does not take drugs, guns and gangs seriously, and they say that gang fighting is normal behavior in their neighborhoods.

Males

A number of items were significantly (p < .05) associated with joining the gang for protection for males, and these are displayed in Table 6. As with the females, some items appear to be contradictory, suggesting again that there may be two types of youths who join gangs for protection -- those who are victims and/or are more law-abiding but fearful and truly want protection, and those who are more aggressive and may join the gang to obtain group backing and support for their activities.

Males for whom protection was important in their decision to join a gang on the one hand were more likely to have been bullied in school, attend church often, be careful to avoid activities that might result in personal injury, never demand that their needs be met and/or to have been forced to have sex that they did not want. On the other hand, others were also more likely to have bullied others in school, say they get what they want even if they have to take it from someone, always engage in activities that might result in personal injury, always demand their needs be met and say they do not believe in God; in fact, they were likely to say they were on Satan's side. Like the females, there appears to be two types of males who join a gang for protection – those who are truly victims and are seeking protection and those who are aggressors and may be seeking peers who engage in similar activities.

TABLE 5

ITEMS SIGNIFICANTLY ASSOCIATED WITH FEMALES FOR WHOM PROTECTION WAS IMPORTANT IN THEIR DECISION TO JOIN A GANG

ITEM	CHI-SQUARE	DF	SIGN
INDIVIDUAL/PEER			
Have been bullied in school	11.907	2	.003
Bullied others in school	9.626	2	.008
Think it's ok to demand that their needs be met	19.939	8	.011
Forced to have unwanted sex	6.568	2	.037
FAMILY			
Parents show favorable attitudes towards drugs, crime and violence	25.717	8	.001
Mother encouraged to join gang	7.040	2	.030
SCHOOL			
School doesn't take drugs, guns and gangs seriously	17.398	8	.026
COMMUNITY			
Gang fights are normal in n'hood	28.359	8	.000

In addition, males who sought protection generally had not completed high school or obtained a GED, were likely to have many close friends in the gang, and they had a tendency to join gangs comprised of only one racial group. For some males, if protection was an important factor in their decision to join the gang, they were likely to have parents who encouraged them to join a gang and who showed favorable attitudes towards drugs, crime and violence. Other males, however, reported that their parents would be embarrassed by their gang membership. These responses may, once again, indicate two different types of youths who are motivated to join the gang for protection.

In terms of their perceptions of their status in their communities, males who joined for protection tend to believe they cannot find a good job and support a family. Further, they are likely to say that gang fighting is considered normal behavior in their neighborhoods and that the schools do not take drugs, guns and gangs seriously. On the other hand, others believe that early intervention with kids would discourage them from joining a gang.

TABLE 6

ITEMS SIGNIFICANTLY ASSOCIATED WITH MALES FOR WHOM PROTECTION WAS IMPORTANT IN THEIR DECISION TO JOIN A GANG

ITEM	CHI-SQUARE	DF	SIGN
INDIVIDUAL/PEER			
Do not believe they will be able to find a good job and support a family	25.681	2	.000
Get what they want even if they have to take it	56.486	8	.000
Bullied by someone in school	33.964	2	.000
Bullied others in school	26.238	2	.000
Often attend church	12.168	2	.002
Always or never engage in activities where they might be injured	47.745	8	.000
Always or never demand their needs be met	33.843	8	.000
Forced to have unwanted sex	39.660	2	.000
Did not complete HS/GED	2.711	2	.002
Do not believe in God	9.835	2	.007
Say they are on Satan's side	7.488	2	.024
Many close friends in the gang	21.851	10	.016
Gang mostly 1 racial group	29.818	4	.000
Family			
Father encouraged to join the gang	51.759	2	.000
Mother encouraged to join the gang	41.939	2	.000
Parents show favorable attitudes towards drugs, crime, violence	101.449	8	.000
Parents would be embarrassed if they knew son was in gang	12.912	2	.002
School			
School does not take involvement with drugs, guns and gangs too seriously	35.322	8	.000
Community			
Gang fighting is normal in n'hood	80.111	8	.000
Believe early intervention would discourage kids from joining	9.930	2	.007

Summary

Again, there is support for the existence of multiple area risk factors. There is similarity between males and females in terms of having what appears to be two different types of youths who join a gang for protection -- victims, or youths who are fearful, and youths who are themselves aggressive and perhaps want group support for their activities. For males, however, additional factors seem to be that they have not completed high school and do not see viable economic opportunities available for them. Perhaps these males do not perceive themselves as being able to make it in the community if left on their own, and/or they may perceive that being involved with the gang is the only realistic economic opportunity they have.

Thus, the hypothesis may be true, at least for some males, that if viable economic alternatives were available, they would not be motivated to join the gang. In addition, different family and community environments might also serve as a deterrent, as both males and females report parents who show favorable attitudes towards drugs, crime and violence, schools that do not take drugs, guns and gangs seriously, and neighborhoods where gang fighting is considered normal.

The Importance of Alternative Social/Recreational Activities

The survey included the retrospective scenario question "if there had been other activities available to you to participate in (for example: sports, music, art, drama, YMCA, Boy's Club, church activities, etc), do you think you would have still joined a gang?" The response modes for this item include: Yes, No, and Not Sure. Some 29% (N = 1124) indicated "no," that if these social opportunities had been available they would not have joined a gang, suggesting that slightly over a fourth "drift" into gangs. Some 35% (N = 1368) indicated "yes," that even if these social opportunities had existed they would have still joined their gang. Finally, some 37% (N = 1453) were "not sure" if they would have still joined a gang if these opportunities had been available. There was no significant difference by gender in response to this variable.

Females

Significant (p < .05) characteristics of females who responded that they would still have joined the gang even if other social/recreational activities had been available to them are listed in Table 7. Females who claim they would still have joined the gang were more likely to say they get what they want even if they have to take it from someone, that they have bullied others, and that they think it is o.k. for them to demand that their needs be met. They were also more likely to say they engage in risky activities where they might be hurt, and that they were still a member of the gang at the time of the survey. These responses suggest that perhaps females with more aggressive, anti-social tendencies are not attracted to more conventional social/recreational activities, anyway, so for them, the availability of alternative activities would not be a deterrent.

Females who still would have joined the gang were more likely to say that their fathers encouraged them to join; however, those who said that their fathers did not encourage them to join were more likely to say they were "not sure" than they were to say "no." Females who said that their mothers encouraged them to join were divided between answering both "yes" and "no" to this question; however, those who said their mothers did not encourage them to join were more likely to answer "not sure" as to whether they would still have joined if other activities were available. Thus, it seems that for females, if their fathers encourage illegal behavior, they are more likely to get involved, but lack of encouragement by their fathers does not guarantee that they will not still get involved. On the other hand, neither encouragement nor lack of encouragement on the part of mothers provides a predictable outcome. Still, females who would still have joined were more likely to say their parents would not be embarrassed by their gang membership, so they do seem to experience some degree of support from their parents for their gang involvement.

Although not displayed in the table, those females who said they would still have joined the gang even if alternative activities were available were more likely to say they had not attempted to quit the gang, nor would they quit the gang if offered a second chance at life. They also said, though, that they did not believe they could quit the gang even if they wanted to, and those who responded that they had tried to quit the gang were more likely to say they were not sure whether they would still have joined if other activities had been available. It is possible, as suggested from these responses, that females may experience some degree of cognitive dissonance once they become involved with a gang. If they do not perceive that they can get out, or if getting out is a negative experience, they may justify staying in by convincing themselves that is where they want to be.

Males

Table 8 lists those characteristics that were significantly associated (p < .05) with males who said they would still have joined the gang even if more conventional alternative social/recreational activities had been available. Males who responded that they would still have joined the gang shared the aggressive, anti-social tendencies of their female counterparts. They were more likely to report that they get what they want even if they have to take it from someone, they were not bullied in school but bullied others, and they do not think bullying leads to gangbanging. They rarely, if ever, attend church and were more likely to say they are not on God's side but are on Satan's side. They tend to engage in risk taking behaviors that could result in personal injury, and they think it is okay to demand that their needs be met. Those who had completed high school or earned their GED were more likely to say they would still have joined the gang, but those who had not were unsure about what decision they would have made. Males who would still have joined the gang in spite of alternative activities being available were also more likely to report having many close friends in the gang and to say that they were currently in the gang at the time of the survey.

TABLE 7

ITEMS SIGNIFICANTLY ASSOCIATED WITH FEMALES WHO WOULD STILL HAVE JOINED A GANG EVEN IF OTHER ALTERNATIVE ACTIVITIES WERE AVAILABLE

ITEM	CHI-SQUARE	DF	SIGN
Individual/Peer			
Get what they want even if they have to take it	22.432	8	.005
Bullied others in school	8.580	2	.014
Engage in risky activities where they could be injured	18.663	8	.017
Think it's ok to demand that their needs be met	24.629	8	.002
Currently a member of the gang	7.875	2	.019
Family			
Father encouraged to join gang	17.148	2	.000
Mother encouraged to join gang	9.101	2	.011
Parents would not be embarrassed if they knew about gang	7.533	2	.023

Males who would still have joined the gang even if alternative activities were available were more likely to say their parents knew about their gang involvement and that both their mothers and fathers had encouraged them to join. Further, they were more likely to report that their parents would not be embarrassed if they knew about their gang involvement and that their parents show favorable attitudes towards drugs, crime and violence. Thus, parents who support and even encourage gang involvement and other illegal behaviors tend to predictably have sons who would choose gang membership over other, more conventional ways to get their social/recreational needs met.

Those males who felt they were not a part of the legitimate opportunity structure in their communities were more likely to say they would still have joined the gang even if other alternative activities were available. These were the males, as indicated previously, who were also more likely to have completed high school or obtained a GED. Given the communities in which these males live, it may well be that they see the gang as offering the best opportunities for them to be successful. These males report that gang fighting is considered normal behavior in their neighborhoods, that their school does not take drugs, guns and gangs seriously, and they know law enforcement officials who are members of a gang. Further, they were more likely to say that they do not think early intervention with kids would discourage them from joining a gang. It appears that these males are enmeshed in a subculture that not only fails to take action against crime, violence, guns and gangs, but that even overtly supports it, as in the case of their parents and law enforcement officials who are, themselves, involved in illegal activities.

TABLE 8

ITEMS SIGNIFICANTLY ASSOCIATED WITH MALES WHO WOULD STILL HAVE JOINED A GANG EVEN IF OTHER ALTERNATIVE ACTIVITIES WERE AVAILABLE

ITEM	CHI-SQUARE	DF	SIGN
INDIVIDUAL/PEER			
Get what they want even if they have to take it	129.607	8	.000
(Not)Bullied in school	6.333	2	.041
Bullied others in school	7.439	2	.024
Do not think bullying leads to gangbanging	26.204	2	.000
Rarely attend church	2.476	2	.002
Engage in risky activities where they might be injured	55.098	8	.000
Think it's ok to demand their needs be met	29.294	8	.000
Completed HS/GED	7.929	2	.019
Say they are on Satan's side	10.308	2	.006
Many close friends in the gang	59.651	10	.000
Currently a gang member	113.141	2	.000
Family			
Parents know about gang membership	68.997	2	.000
Father encouraged to join the gang	10.912	2	.004
Mother encouraged to join the gang	11.616	2	.003
Parents show favorable attitudes towards drugs, crime, violence	20.313	8	.009
Parents would not be embarrassed if they knew son was in gang	59.353	2	.000
School			
School does not take involvement with drugs, guns and gangs too seriously	17.004	8	.030

TABLE 8:	**Continued**		
ITEM	CHI-SQUARE	DF	SIGN
Community			
Do not feel part of legitimate opportunity structure	6.731	2	.034
Gang fighting is normal in n'hood	65.980	8	.000
Say they know law enforcement officials who are in gang	10.617	2	.005
Don't believe early intervention discourages kids from joining	76.402	2	.000

Summary

For this variable, there were not significant differences between males and females. There was, once more, support for the belief that risk factors appear in several different aspects of youths' lives, and for this variable, that was more evident for males than females. The findings related to this variable suggest that while there are some youths who might be deterred from joining a gang if other, more conventional alternatives were available, there are others for whom the presence of alternatives would not make a difference. For those youths, especially males, who tend to display aggressive, anti-social characteristics to begin with, then who are surrounded by friends, family, schools and a larger community that overtly or covertly supports involvement in illegal activities, and who further see no viable legitimate opportunities for themselves, gang involvement may be perceived as the most rational choice for survival and success.

The good news from the results of the analysis of this variable, though, is that there are more than 25% of youths who join gangs who replied on the survey that they would not have joined had other alternative activities been available. It also seems that these youths have other factors that work in their favor as well, such as less aggressive personalities, fewer gang involved friends, parents who are opposed to involvement in illegal activities and perceptions that their communities do not consider involvement in crime, drugs, guns and gangs the norm. They are also more likely to believe that early intervention efforts might, indeed, discourage kids from joining a gang. For these youths, clearly, an investment in conventional social/recreational alternatives could result in keeping them out of gang life.

CONCLUSION

While some differences between males and females were noted, there were also many similarities. For those youths for whom money was an important factor in their decision to join a gang, males generally exhibited more anti-social characteristics than females. They also tended to consider economic factors more so than females in their decision to join a gang, such as whether they have access to legitimate opportunities and/or whether they will be able to get a good job and support a family. In addition, educational status appeared to be a more important factor for males than females.

Although protection appeared to be a more important reason overall to join a gang for females than males, there seemed to be two different groups within each gender who joined a gang for protection -- victims and aggressors. And for those youths who joined a gang due to a lack of available alternative activities, males appeared to be more anti-social, more immersed in a delinquent subculture, and, again, more motivated by economic concerns. For both males and females, risk factors were present in all major facets of their lives, although how many risk factors and how many life components varied somewhat by gender on the different variables.

The hypothesis that youths would be less likely to join gangs if other positive alternative activities were available to them received mixed support from the results of this study. If the primary motivation for joining a gang is making money, and youths do not perceive that they have the necessary skills and opportunities to make money through legitimate means, then the gang may be the only viable route to economic success they see. If that is the case, then they will be determined to go that route. Two different groups of youths tend to say they joined the gang for protection -- one group being fearful and/ or actual victims, the other being aggressors. It seems likely that if other support mechanisms were available in the family, schools and/or communities, then those youths who are fearful and/or victims might perceive that they could get their needs better met outside of the gang. The aggressors, however, may be seeking group support and/or protection in the sense that there is safety in numbers. More conventional activities may not have much of a deterrent effect for those youths. Thus, if the primary motivation to join a gang is for protection, then the level of involvement in and commitment to the gang may vary depending on whether the person perceives that he or she has any viable alternatives for getting his or her needs met elsewhere.

Youths may also join gangs because there is a lack of any positive alternatives for meeting their social/recreational needs. According to the results of this survey, this was the case for more than one-fourth of the youths who had joined a gang. These youths do not exhibit anti-social characteristics, nor do they appear to be submerged in the delinquent/criminal subculture. Further, although not displayed in the table, when they do join a gang, they tend to remain somewhat peripheral and perceive that they can quit when they want to. Basically, they do not seem to take on "gang member" as an identity for themselves. For this group of young people, it seems that having positive alternative activities available could realistically prevent them from becoming involved in gangs. These youths appear to be salvageable, and it would make sense to target that group in future prevention/intervention efforts.

The findings from this study indicate that prevention/early intervention efforts could be effective in deterring at least some youths from joining gangs. Basically, positive alternative social/recreational activities, resources to provide support and protection to youths who are fearful and/or being victimized, programs to encourage school completion, and viable economic opportunities for older teens could result in fewer youths joining gangs to get their needs met in these areas. In addition, the results suggest that interventions to deal with early anti-social behavior and instill basic values could be helpful as well. Other interventions that strengthen core social institutions are needed, too, such that families, schools and communities work together to provide clear limits and expectations regarding law-abiding behavior and provide immediate and consistent sanctions when the expected behavior fails to occur. In essence, since risk factors permeate all components of a youth's life, prevention/intervention efforts need to do the same in order to be effective. Following are more specific suggested interventions in each major area:

Individual/Peer
Teach children moral, spiritual and civic values.
Teach children impulse control and stress management skills.
Teach children pro-social and other critical life skills.
Provide children with positive adult role models.
Encourage children to develop friendships with non-delinquent peers.

Family
Support programs that strengthen families and promote healthy
growth and development of children and adolescents.
Teach parenting skills.
Support activities to promote bonding between parents and children.
Teach families non-violent conflict resolution skills
Parents need to model and give children clear, consistent messages
regarding expected pro-social behavior.

School
Intervene at earliest signs of anti-social behavior.
Include alcohol/drug and violence prevention programs with regular
curriculum.
Develop interventions to reduce truancy.
Increase school discipline and give students clear, consistent
anti-drugs/guns/gangs/messages.
Provide targeted literacy programs in early grades.
Provide after school programs/extracurricular activities for
latchkey children.
Develop interventions to improve high school completion.

Community
Provide safe, secure environment for children.
Provide opportunities for children and adolescents to participate
in community activities to develop a sense of importance and belonging.
Provide internship/apprenticeship opportunities to help youths
transition from school to work.
Provide comprehensive health and social services to youths in format that is

easily accessible, affordable and user friendly.
Provide positive adult role models and clear, consistent
anti-drugs/guns/gangs messages.
Encourage more pro-social programming by various media.

This is by no means an exhaustive list, but a few suggestions that can make a difference. There are children who can be helped and there are ways to help them; the test will be whether we as a society have the will and commitment to take action.

REFERENCES

Cohen, Albert K. 1955. *Delinquent boys*. Glencoe: Free Press.

Hawkins, J. David and Richard F. Catalano. 1992. *Communities that care*. San Francisco: Jossey-Bass.

Hawkins, J. David and Richard F. Catalano. 1993. *Risk-focused prevention using the social development strategy*. Seattle, WA: Developmental Research and Programs, Inc.

Hawkins, J. David, Richard F. Catalano and J.Y. Miller. 1992. Risk and protective factors for alcohol and other drug problems in adolescence and early adulthood: Implications for substance abuse prevention. *Psychological Bulletin*, 112:64-105.

Hirschi, Travis. 1969. *Causes of delinquency*. Berkeley: University of California Press.

Hochhaus, C. and F. Sousa. 1988. Why children belong to gangs: A comparison of expectations and reality. *The High School Journal*, December - January:74-77.

Jankowski, Martin Sanchez. 1990. *Islands in the street: Gangs and American urban society*. Berkeley, CA: University of California Press.

Merton, Robert K. 1938. Social structure and anomie. *American Sociological Review*, 3:672-82.

Miller, Walter. 1958. Lower-class culture as a generating milieu of gang delinquency. *Journal of Social Issues*, 14:5-19.

Padilla, Felix M. 1992. *The gang as an American enterprise*. New Brunswick,NJ: Rutgers University Press.

Reiner, I. 1992. *Gangs, crime and violence in Los Angeles: Findings and proposals from the District Attorney's office.* Arlington, VA: National Youth Gang Information Center.

Shaw, Clifford R. And Henry D. McKay. 1942. *Juvenile delinquency and urban areas.* Chicago: University of Chicago Press.

Spergel, Irving A. and G. David Curry. 1992. The National Youth Gang Survey: A research and development process. In A. Goldstein and C.R. Huff (Eds.), *Gang Intervention Handbook.* Champaign-Urbana: Academic Press.

Sutherland, Edwin. 1939. *Principles of criminology.* Philadelphia: Lippincott.

Vigil, James Diego. 1988. *Barrio gangs.* Austin: University of Texas Press.

CHAPTER SIX

THE GIRLS CLUB

Kathleen Aquino, M.P.H.
Los Padrinos Juvenile Hall

This chapter will describe trends in female involvement in the juvenile justice system and the behaviors of female adolescent gang members. It will also describe the characteristics and motivations of this misunderstood population. As most detained gang members are male, not much information has been collected regarding female gang members. The chapter includes some of the findings about female gang members from the Project GANGFACT study sponsored by the National Gang Crime Research Center. More than one thousand females participated in the Project GANGFACT study, which surveyed confined offenders from 17 different states. Although the majority of the information presented focuses on female gang members, comparisons are made between males and females and female gang vs. non-gang members on some items. Specifically, this chapter covers the following areas of interest:

1. History and trends of females involved with the juvenile justice system,
2. Description of female gang members: behavior and background, and
3. Factors that influence female gang membership.

Trends in the Number of Females Arrested in the United States

During the 12 months ending June 30, 1996, the number of women under the jurisdiction of State and Federal prison authorities grew from 69,161 to 73,607, an increase of 6.4%. The number of men rose 5.2%, from 1,036,390 to 1,090,749. At midyear 1996, women accounted for 6.3% of all prisoners nationwide, increasing from 5.7% in 1990, and 4.1% in 1980 (Gilliard and Beck, 1997).

At the largest juvenile detention facility in Southern California, the number of female detainees has noticeably increased. Five years ago, one building housed about sixty young women. Now there are three buildings that house about 120 detainees. This doubling of the female population corresponds with the higher percentage of juvenile females detained in the County of Los Angeles, which has risen from approximately nine to 16% of the detention population.

According to data provided by the Uniform Crime Reports, United States law enforcement agencies made approximately 748,000 arrests involving females under the age of 18 in 1997, representing 26% of all juvenile arrests made that year. The proportion of juvenile arrests accounted for by females has risen gradually over the past ten years, as girls comprised 22% of all juvenile arrests in 1986 (Chesney-Lind and Shelden, 1998). Although there has also been an increase in the number of males arrested, between 1993 and 1997, increases in arrests were greater, or decreases smaller, for girls than for boys in almost every offense category (Snyder, 1999). More distressing than their increasing numbers is the more serious nature of their crimes. Between 1981 and 1997, the female juvenile arrest rate for serious violent crimes rose 103%, compared to a 27% increase for boys during that same period (Snyder, 1999).

The Office of Juvenile Justice and Delinquency Prevention (1997) notes the following three trends in the arrests and detention of girls since 1989. First, arrests and petitions to court for robbery and aggravated assault have increased. Second, the age of initial involvement in the justice system is getting younger, with a 10% increase in the number of 13 and 14-year-olds entering juvenile court. And third, representation of African-American females has increased over the past five years from 17% to 22%. In a report comprised of information from almost 30 states, the National Council on Crime and Delinquency reports that almost 50% of all girls in secure detention are African-American. Hispanics and Caucasians account for 13% and 34% respectively. The article asserts that, "if these trends continue, female delinquents will continue to occupy more time and attention of policy makers, service providers, court officials, law enforcement agencies, and communities" (OJJDP, 1997).

The History of Females in the Juvenile Justice System in the United States

In 1823, the Society for the Reformation of Juvenile Delinquents began to manage "juvenile delinquents." These included homeless children and children from "unfit homes." The term "unfit home" had no established definition, so the circumstances involved with the removal of these children remains unclear. The society described these children as "beyond control" and "incorrigible" (Brown, 1993).

About 30 years later, in 1856, The Society for the Reformation of Juvenile Delinquency established the first reform school for girls in Massachusetts. The superintendent of the reform school described the ethnic/racial background of the first 100 girls as native born (53%) and immigrant (47%). Half of all females were not arrested by the police but instead brought in by relatives who deemed the girls "wayward," "deceitful," "wanton and loud," and "idle." Many of the immigrant females were from economically deprived homes and had to work to help the family. These immigrants were viewed as "too independent." They used the streets to get to and from work and sometimes had to travel alone. Wealthier families did not relate with young women walking the streets alone, never mind working (Brown, 1993).

Early detention facilities were run military style and included solitary confinement. No school lessons or work training was provided. In other facilities, the youth were used as child labor in nearby factories. Seventy years later, in 1899, the first Juvenile Court was established in Chicago.

In the early 1900s, American society was concerned with promiscuity and other status offenses on the part of girls. For example, many girls found to be having sex were placed into reform schools. In the early 20th century, more girls were incarcerated in reform schools than boys. Between 1910-1920, 23 facilities were built to provide protection for these "delinquent" girls. The Los Angeles County Juvenile Court system was established in 1903, and because of the high number of female detainees, was managed and supervised by a woman correctional officer (Brown, 1993). Even though the nature of female juvenile offending has changed over the past few decades, a far greater number of girls have always come to the attention of the juvenile justice system for status and other minor offenses compared to their male counterparts.

Does the Juvenile Justice System Treat Female Adolescents Differently?
The Office of Juvenile Justice and Delinquency Prevention (1997) reports that more girls than boys continue to be incarcerated for status offenses. Status offenses include crimes of incorrigible behavior, running away, and truancy. These status charges are duplicated in a trend called "bootstrapping." In these situations, the original charges brought against the female are layered with new charges such as missing a court appearance. In a study conducted in Florida in the early 1990's, Bishop and Frazier (1991) found that in the juvenile justice system, "adolescents more likely to be bootstrapped were females who had committed status offenses. This leads to more serious charges and time brought against the girls, whose punishment outweighed the seriousness of their offenses."

Girls Inc., a national youth organization, provides information regarding the treatment of female juvenile detainees. According to their recent publication, "Prevention & Parity: Girls in Juvenile Justice," a lack of research information and gender inequality have made attempts at rehabilitation ineffective. Although more males than females pass through the system, females are treated unfairly and more severely. Ironically, most crimes committed by females are much less serious than those committed by male offenders. As mentioned above, the girls are mostly charged with running away, truancy, and being out after curfew.

The report further asserts that girls are "more than twice as likely to be detained before a hearing and are detained on average three to five times longer than their male counterparts. Detention before a hearing is twice as likely to result in out-of-home placement for girls than for boys." Isabel Carter Stewart, National Executive Director of Girls Inc., contends that "for many girls, the juvenile justice system is their last, best hope for rehabilitation and we must make it responsive to their needs."

Because the majority of law enforcement officers, probation officers, correctional officers, and judges are men, communication problems and misunderstandings are bound to occur. Additionally, cultural incompetence may result in misjudging a female arrestee based on her own beliefs. Girls who lack the confidence to express themselves clearly may avoid communication altogether. Similarly, those who fear confrontation may not have the ability to assert themselves or explain their situation. Conversely, girls who have been taught to stand up for themselves may be seen as aggressive, difficult, or uncooperative. As a result, rather than have juvenile justice system personnel be responsive to their needs, these girls may find that they are treated more harshly. Given the behavior of girls involved in gangs, many may find themselves in that situation.

Description of Female Gang Members -- Behavior and Background Variables

The following data are from the Project GANGFACT study conducted by the National Gang Crime Research Center in 1995. This study involved an anonymous survey of juveniles and young adults in a variety of correctional programs and facilities in 17 different states. Approximately 10,000 young people participated in the survey, with about 4,000 self-reporting that they were or had previously been gang members. Since some of the programs and facilities included in the study contained females, data from the study were analyzed to examine gang involvement by young women, compare gang and non-gang females on certain items, and compare gang involved females with gang involved males.

For a more complete description of Project GANGFACT and the methodology for the study, please refer to Chapters One and Two of this monograph, or contact the National Gang Crime Research Center for a copy of the full report.

Demographics
    There were 1,058 females included in the survey. The racial/ethnic breakdown for all female participants was as follows: African American n = 497 (47%), White/Caucasian n = 381 (36%), Latino n = 89 (8%), Asian/ Chinese n = 13 (1%), American Indian n = 27 (3%), Arab American n = 19 (2%), and Other n = 32 (3%).
    Approximately one-third of the females stated that they were or had been members of a gang (n = 311). Of those female respondents who identified themselves as gang members, the racial/ethnic breakdown was as follows: African American n = 146 (47%), White/Caucasian n = 73 (24%), Latino n = 50 (16%), Asian/Chinese n = 11 (4%), American Indian n = 7 (2%), Arab American n = 8 (3%), and Other n = 16 (5%). In comparing male with female gang members by race/ethnic identity, most groups are equivalent. There are two group exceptions -- Asian/Chinese, where the number of males is more than six times that of females, and Arab-American, where the number of females is five times that of their male counterparts.
    In examining Table 1, it may be inferred that if Asian, Latino, Other, or Arab American females are detained, the chance of them belonging to a gang is higher than expected. This concept may, to some extent, be explained culturally. Generally, Asians and Latinos are group oriented and interdependent, while White/Anglo and African Americans are more independent.

Table 1
Gang Affiliation by Race/Ethnicity
For Females In Detention

Race/Ethnicity	Observed	Expected	+/- (ratio of obs/exp)
Asian/Chinese	11	3.7	+2.97
Latino/Hispanic	50	26.0	+1.92
White/Caucasian	73	111.6	- 0.65
African American	146	145.6	Equivalent
Other	16	9.4	+1.70
Arab American	8	5.6	+1.43
American Indian	7	7.9	-0.88

    It may be that group cohesiveness leads to more peer pressure and vulnerability to gang membership. Although the numbers of some groups represented are small, one would expect the distribution of gang involved girls to be similar to their representation in the total sample. In Table 1, the number of girls expected to answer "yes" to gang membership is illustrated. The largest ratio between observed and expected results was among Asian females (2.97 times), with Latinos (1.92 times) second, the "Other" category (1.7 times) third, and Arab-Americans (1.43 times) fourth. The number of African American females equals that which was expected. As for White/ Caucasian females, there was a lower than expected value for involvement in gang activity (-0.65 times), and the same was true with American Indian females (-0.88 times).

Thus, of all female participants, the racial/ethnic groups most involved with gang activity are: Asian/Chinese (85%), Latino (56%), Other (50%), and Arab American (42%). In contrast, the groups of females least involved with gangs are: African American (29%), American Indian (26%), and White/ Caucasian (19%).

Living Arrangements

In the Knox et al. (1997) survey, living arrangements of gang members were compared by gender. Most living situations were similar for both males and females. A similar proportion of males (35%) and females, (32%) reported that they lived with "mother, father and siblings," while slightly more males (57% vs. 55%) than females reported living with "mother and siblings." The largest difference was noted between those who said that they lived with "father and siblings," which was 9% for males and 13% for females. Differences in living arrangements between males and females were slightly statistically significant (Chi-square = 6.68, p=.035).

In comparing the living arrangements of gang and non-gang female members, 43% of those who were non-gang involved reported living with both parents and siblings, with 51% living with "mother and siblings," and 6% with "father and siblings." In contrast, 32% of gang involved females reported living with "mother, father and siblings," while 55% said they were living with "mother and siblings," and 13% were living with "father and siblings." The differences in living situations between gang and non-gang females were statistically significant (Chi-square =19.6, p <.001). So, although most detained adolescents in this study live in an environment where the mother is the head of the household, gang involved females reside in homes where the mother is absent one and one-half times more than gang involved males and twice more than non-gang involved females.

The Role of the Female Gang Member

Some respondents provided information in addition to what was asked in the survey questions. Among other things, this information offered a glimpse into female gang activity. Female gang members have clearly defined roles in the gang. If she is in a position of authority, she will do her best to take care of her responsibilities. If she is incarcerated and unable to deal with problems, she will enlist the help of other members. One youth shared this situation as an example of how her authority was just as strong "inside" as "on the outs." This young woman had heard that her "home girls" were not doing enough work out on the streets. She referred to drug selling and other work to generate money for the gang. She asked a couple of the male gang members to rough the girls up and remind them to get back to work. The female workers were also instructed to give the money earned to the "gang mom." The "gang mom" is described as an older female who has been in the gang for a long time. "Older" is described as "older than thirty." The males did as they were asked and the problem was solved. Thus, although young and incarcerated, this female gang leader was able to "take care of business."

Within the gang, most female gang members do not usually hold positions of authority. Those who have authority do not put themselves out on the street. Most female gang members' duties include hiding money and weapons on themselves (they are less likely to be searched by the police), selling drugs, and obtaining information from males in rival gangs.

Some females, however, are involved in many of the same activities as the male members, such as driving the car and even pulling the trigger during a drive-by shooting. In the Knox et al. (1997) study, 77% of the females responded that "there are female leaders in their gang." When males were asked the same question, only 43% agreed. Just over half (51%) of females surveyed reported that they have "ever held rank or any leadership position in the gang" compared with about 61% of the males, a difference that was statistically significant (Chi-square=9.95, p=.002). About 76% of female respondents stated that they "had met face-to-face with the top leader of their gang," versus 67% of the males. That difference was also statistically significant (Chi-square=10.6, p=.001).

Spiritual & Religious Beliefs

There is very little information available on the spiritual beliefs of gang members. Even less is known about female gang members. Additionally, scant information is known regarding church attendance and if they believe in God. A few questions on the survey, however, did provide information on religious beliefs. More female non-gang members than gang members reported that they "often attended church" (53% vs. 45%), which was a significant difference (Chi-square=5.94, p=.015). More than three times as many female gang members as non-gang members reported that they "do not believe in God" (12% vs. 4%), also a significant difference (Chi-square=25.8, p<.001). Similarly, 13% of female gang members agreed with the statement, "I'm on Satan's side," compared with 3% of non-gang affiliated females (Chi-square=35.2, p<.001).

Drug Selling Behavior

When asked if they had been "involved in organized drug dealing," three-fourths of those who were gang involved answered affirmatively, while only 32% of non-gang involved girls agreed. The difference between the two groups was statistically significant (Chi-square=174.0, p<.001). Nearly twice as many (63%) gang involved girls had sold cocaine as non-gang involved girls (32%), and that difference was also significant (Chi-square=94.9, p<.001). More than four times as many gang involved girls reported that they "had tried to smuggle any illegal drugs into the facility where they were presently incarcerated" (23% vs. 5%), which was a significant difference (Chi-square=70.1, p<.001).

Weapon Acquisition and Use

As expected, more male gang members than female gang members admitted "firing a gun at a police officer" (32% vs. 20%), a statistically significant difference (Chi-square=20.5, p<.001). When compared with other females, however, female gang members were five times more likely than non-gang members to report that they had fired a gun at a police officer (20% vs. 4%), also statistically significant (Chi-square=75.8, p<.001). Further, more gang members (44%) reported that "since March 1994 it has been easier to buy illegal guns" compared with non-gang members (32%), a significant difference (Chi-square=10.9, p=.004).

Access to and use of weapons is common among juvenile offenders generally, not only gang members. Ash, Kellerman, Fuqua-Whitley and Johnson (1996) conducted a study to learn more about gun acquisition and use by juvenile offenders. They interviewed juvenile offenders ages 13 - 18 in detention centers in Atlanta, Georgia. The average age was 15.7 years. They found that 65% of males and nearly 20% of female youths had owned a gun. Eighty-four percent of gun carriers got their first gun before the age of 15 years; more than half received their first gun passively, without any specific plan to do so. Those who actively got their first gun tended to carry it with them more often, with some doing so constantly. Almost half (40%) said they felt more energized, excited, and powerful while carrying the gun, but most also indicated that they felt anxiety about getting caught with the gun. A similar study conducted by Durant, Getts, Cadenhead and Woods (1995) found that although males were more likely to carry a hidden weapon than females, females who carried weapons were more likely than males to be involved in gang fights. Conversely, males who carried a weapon with them were more likely to attack someone with whom they lived.

Mental Health/Social Support

Leaders in the juvenile justice field frequently raise concerns about the mental health problems of youths served in their facilities and programs. One issue that has been addressed is the lack of social support in the lives of juvenile offenders. In one study, Lewandowski & Westman, (1996) compared adolescents who were court referred to a delinquency prevention program (n = 34) to a control group (n = 89). The students in the program reported that they were "more likely to receive the social support that they wanted." Those students involved with the court referred program also had lower rates of recidivism. The decrease in repeat arrests and "admitting their need for support" reveals that these youth were ready to receive support.

In another study, Anderson (1994) found that of all groups studied and respondents who gave suggestions for the kind of help teenagers need, the most common response was "someone to listen and to care." Because these youth also indicated the critical importance of social support, it is essential that intervention programs contain a social support component.

Another issue is the existence of identifiable mental/emotional disorders among juvenile offenders. Timmons-Mitchell, Brown, Schulz, Webster,

Underwood and Semple (1997) evaluated the prevalence of mental disorders among youth detained in juvenile detention facilities. The mental health needs of male and female adolescents were compared. The females displayed significantly more mental health needs than the males. The estimated prevalence of mental disorders for boys was 27%, compared with 84% for females.

Another study (Casper, Belanoff and Offer, 1996) described gender differences in psychiatric symptoms and their relationship to less serious delinquent behavior. A survey was administered to nearly 500 students. Using a series of psychological and delinquency testing instruments, the 249 male and 248 female students rated themselves. Female adolescents of all races reported much higher levels of emotional distress, in particular a depressed mood and anxiety, than did male adolescents. Trouble paying attention in school and marijuana, alcohol, and other drug use were associated with higher levels of psychiatric symptoms. African American and White/Caucasian adolescents were similar in psychological adjustment.

Lie and Wagner (1996) provided insight into female delinquency through a study of a combined sample of delinquent and non-delinquent girls. A prospective analysis was conducted with more than 2,000 young girls and female adolescents, in which the subjects were followed for about 10 years. At follow-up, 80 of the subjects had committed crimes serious enough to be entered on the General Police Register. These young women offenders were then matched by age with non-offenders, and the two groups were compared using quantitative testing instruments. Significant differences were found for the Tension and Pathology scores, suggesting that these young females were characterized as "youngsters having anxiety and other forms of psychopathology rather than innate hostility."

Since most detained youth are males, service providers may have difficulties addressing and meeting the needs of female youth. The lack of mental health professionals available and the high number of detained youth are but two reasons for this. Another may be that generally, the time youths spend in juvenile detention facilities is quite short, often only 2-3 weeks. In one juvenile detention hall in Southern California, nearly 600 youths are served by only one part-time (20% time) psychiatrist, and four clinical social workers. Thus, the combination of multiple youths moving in and out of a facility in a brief period of time and mental health staff who are only there on a limited basis makes it difficult to provide adequate services.

Behavior of Females Incarcerated in a Juvenile Detention Facility

In the study conducted by Knox et al. (1997), female gang and non-gang members who were incarcerated were compared in terms of behaviors that might result in disciplinary action by facility staff. Females who admitted to gang membership reported higher frequencies of fighting, threatening injury to others, smuggling drugs, and weapon possession while incarcerated. When asked, "how many disciplinary reports have you had while in this facility," 28% of gang members answered that they had had five or more reports filed compared with 12% of the non-gang members who had had that many, a statistically significant difference (Chi-square=70.1, p<.001). Forty-seven percent of the gang members had "been in a fight with someone while in this facility," versus 20% of non-gang involved girls, also a significant difference (Chi-square=76.3, p<.001). Thirty-two percent of the female gang members reported that they had "started a fight or attacked someone while in this facility," compared to 9% of those not in a gang, a significant difference (Chi-square=84.4, p<.001). A quarter of all female gang members admitted to carrying a homemade weapon (knife, etc.) while in the facility, while only 6% of the non-gang females had done the same; this difference, too, was significant (Chi-square=65.8, p<.001). When asked if they had threatened any staff member or officer while in the facility, nearly one-third (31%) of the female gang members answered "yes" compared to 9% of non-gang members, with the difference reaching statistical significance (Chi-square=82.7, p<.001).

When asked if gangs use religion as a "front" in order to do business, the results were comparable for both gang and non-gang members, 30% and 22% respectively, although the difference was slightly statistically significant (Chi-square=5.56, p=.018). The girls who were gang members were also more likely to say they had tried to smuggle illegal drugs into the facility than were their non-gang counterparts (23% vs. 5%), clearly a significant difference (Chi-square=70.1, p<.001).

There were similar views among the two groups (gang members vs. non-gang members) toward gang recruitment within a correctional center. When asked if they thought that a zero tolerance approach to gang activity would affect gang recruitment, 65% of the female gang members reported that there would be "no effect," while 56% of non-gang females agreed, only a slightly significant difference (Chi-square=6.51, p=.011). Not surprisingly, 63% of female gang members thought that there was a connection between adult prison gangs and juvenile correctional institution gangs, but 48% of the non-gang members thought so as well, again a slightly significant difference (Chi-square=15.0, p=.001).

These results are compared in Table 2.

TABLE 2

Comparison of Rule-Violating Behaviors in Juvenile Correctional Facilities by Female Gang and Non-Gang Members

Survey Item	Non gang	Gang
Have had five (5) or more disciplinary reports while in facility	12%	28%
Has been in a physical fight with anyone while in facility?	20%	47%
Started a fight or attacked someone while in facility?	9%	32%
Has carried a homemade weapon (knife, etc.) while in facility	6%	25%
Has threatened any facility staff member or officer while in facility	9%	31%
Has tried to smuggle any illegal drugs while in facility?	5%	23%
Agrees that gangs use religion as a "front" in order to do business in facility?	22%	30%
Thinks that a zero tolerance approach to gang activity within a correctional facility affects gang recruitment	56%	65%
Thinks there is a connection between adult prison gangs and juvenile institutional gangs?	48%	63%

What Motivates Females to Join a Gang?

In order to address the problem of gang involvement, we must understand factors that influence a young woman's decision to join a gang. Research on female delinquents and professionals who work with delinquent girls agree that some of the factors that may lead to gang involvement include a lack of family support, violence in the home, and familial involvement in gangs. Additionally, components that influence female juvenile arrests in general include parental neglect, drug and alcohol abuse, physical abuse, and difficulties with school. Many girls in the peer group of the gang members are also likely to share these problems. Some reasons females have given for joining a gang are for protection, social interaction, money, and the sense of family and affiliation.

In more recent years, if females are unable to get those needs met within a co-ed gang, they are increasingly likely to form gangs of their own. Along with the positive elements of psycho-social need fulfillment, however, these all female gangs are also engaging in crime such as is typical with more traditional male dominated gangs, and some experts believe that this phenomenon will become more common. "Female gangs are beginning to evolve exclusively of male dominated gangs. These gangs will emerge as independent criminal elements, and female gang members will become more involved in gang violence and other criminally oriented activities" (electric.ss.uci.edu/~rickg/gangs2000/executive.html).

Molidor (1996) compiled a report from interviews with female gang members representing several gangs in Texas and New Mexico. They had each been arrested one to six times. When asked what the appeal of gang membership was, they reported: "the sense of belonging to a family; power, protection, and respect based on the fear that the gang inspired in others. These females also said they feared violence and sexual abuse from members of their own gang." Female gang members may be a replacement for their male counterparts who are incarcerated, injured (either temporarily or permanently) or deceased. One may also view the increase in female gang members as a remnant of the social changes that have expanded women's roles in society.

Lack of Family Support and Violence in the Home

Recently, more attention has been focused on girls in the juvenile justice system. A general finding from a variety of sources is that female juvenile delinquents, and especially female gang members, tend to come from seriously dysfunctional families. Female juvenile offenders are, on average, 15 to 16 years of age and from low socioeconomic communities. These girls tend to be high school dropouts and many have been victims of sexual and/or physical abuse. Half as many gang members (21%) have completed high school/GED compared with non- gang members (50%) (Knox et al., 1997). In addition, many come from single parent families, have experienced foster care placement, lack adequate work and social skills, and are substance abusers.

In a survey conducted with 305 subjects, Chang (1996) found that "female gang members show a high profile of family dysfunction. Female gang members were significantly more likely to have histories of childhood abuse than non-gang members. They were more likely to report that they had been mentally or sexually abused, and had been neglected by their parents. Also, more gang members than non-gang members reported a bad relationship with their mothers and fathers." According to Knox et al. (1997), 33% of female gang members said that my parents "never or rarely" knew where I was and whom I was with, compared to18% of non-gang members who gave that response. Conversely, more than half (55%) of the non-gang females reported that their parents "always or usually knew" where they were and whom they were with, compared with 38% of female gang members. These differences were statistically significant (Chi-square=17.4, p=.002).

Michael Males's book (1996), *The Scapegoat Generation: America's War on Adolescents*, provides insight into the concept of parental support. Males reports that Americans 35 and older account for more than 40% of emergency room visits involving cocaine and that from 1980 to 1995 there was a 76% increase in violent crime arrests of those ages 30 to 45. He states, "Kids today are being raised by the most violent, drug-abusing parents in history."   Although one illustration does not imply a general trend, a particular 16-year-old reported that the reason she had joined a gang was that her stepfather had physically abused her. She ran away and told male gang member friends about the abuse. They promised to protect her. When asked if they did protect her, she proudly and happily replied that "yes, they did."

Parental Incarceration

Another issue recently brought to light is the high level of incarceration of parents of youth in the juvenile justice system. It is estimated that between one and two million children have at least one parent in prison at any given time (Christopher Commission, 1991). Many more children have experienced the imprisonment of a parent at some point over the course of their young lives.   According to a 1993 study, these children are much "more likely to become incarcerated than children of parents who never spent time behind bars." Even if not arrested, the "negative effects on children of parental arrest include traumatic stress, loneliness, developmental regression, loss of self-confidence, aggression, withdrawal, depression, interpersonal violence, substance abuse, and teenage pregnancy" (Donziger, 1996).   This reality was supported by the Knox et al. (1997) survey results, which found that more than twice as many (44% vs. 19%) female gang members as non-gang members reported that their parents had ever served time in prison. This difference was statistically significant (Chi1square=62.7, p<.001).

In 1996, the number of women in prison rose by 9.1 percent, nearly double the increase of male prisoners. At year-end, 74,730 women were in State or Federal prison, accounting for 6.3% of inmates nationwide (Bureau of Justice Statistics, 1996).   An analysis of the female prison population (Snell and Morton, 1994) found that nearly 80% of women incarcerated in state prisons have children. The 25,714 mothers in prison had more than 56,000 children under age 18. African American (69%) and Hispanic (72%) female inmates were more likely than white (62%) women to have children under age 18. African American women were slightly more likely than other women to have lived with their young children before entering prison. Nearly 10% of the women prisoners reported that their children were in a foster home, agency, or institution. The Christopher Commission Report (1991) further pointed out that only 9% of women inmates at the state level receive visits from their minor children, largely because most state prisons for women are geographically isolated. As a result of this lack of contact, even if their children are in trouble, incarcerated mothers may not even know.

In addition to their parents, many children have other relatives who have been incarcerated as well. The incarceration of other family members may also disproportionately affect females. For example, Snell and Morton (1994) found that women in prison were more likely than male inmates to have had at least one member of their immediate family who had been incarcerated (47% vs. 37%). About 35% of the women had a brother and 10% had a sister who had served a jail or prison sentence. Higher percentages of African American women than Anglo women had family members that had been in jail or prison. For example, 42% of African American, 36% of Hispanic, and 26% of Anglo inmates reported that a brother had been incarcerated, and 11% of Anglo women and 5% of African American women had a father who had served jail or prison time (Snell and Morton, 1994).

Family and Friends as Gang Members

According to Chang (1996), "as expected, female gang members were significantly more likely to report that they had parents, brothers or sisters in gangs (44.2% vs. 18.5%), and boyfriends in gangs (76.2% vs. 31.3%) than non-gang members. Overwhelmingly, gang members had male friends in gangs (91.8% vs. 60.1%) and female friends in gangs (78.9% vs. 34.7%)." In some cases, youth not officially in a gang also have friends who are gang involved, as indicated by findings from the Knox et al. (1997) survey. When asked how many of their close friends and associates were gang members, 15% of the non-gang members and 77% of the gang members answered, "five or more," a statistically significant difference (Chi-square=414.2, p<.001).

Drug and Alcohol Abuse

According to a survey conducted by the Bureau of Justice Statistics (1996), a third of female inmates said that a parent or guardian had abused drugs or alcohol while the inmate was growing up. Alcohol was more often cited than drugs, as 32% of the women had a parent who abused alcohol, while only 7% had a parent that abused drugs. Of white women in prison, 42% reported parental abuse of drugs or alcohol, compared to 33% of Hispanic women and 26% of African American women.

The Chang (1996) study cited earlier also found that more female adolescent gang members than non-gang members reported having mothers with drinking problems. During an interview with a young girl of fifteen, she stated that her older brother, also a gang member, forbade her to use drugs or alcohol. The brother, described as "big and built," had spread the word that if anyone was caught giving the girl drugs or liquor, that person would seriously regret it. The minor reported that she had developed relationships outside of the gang because she liked to "party and get high sometimes." As her brother had a position of authority in the gang and had warned the other members not to give his sister drugs or alcohol, she was chastised for even asking for them.

Violence, Aggression, and Bullying

Although no one argues that females are becoming more involved in violence, there is a wide range of opinions regarding female aggression. While historically research studies have shown that males are infinitely more violent and aggressive, more recent studies report that the rate of violence perpetrated by women is increasing. This was illustrated in the increase of females arrested for violent crimes discussed earlier. Other professionals interviewed for this section describe the increase in female violence and female arrests as "expected." Some postulate that the violence is an artifact of the women's movement and societal changes in the way we view women. Another interviewee mused that because women are not yet comfortable with acting out violent behavior, they tend to react swiftly and deliberately to ensure the act is complete.

Some researchers suggest that early bullying behavior may be an indicator of later violence. In addition, findings from the Knox et al. (1997) survey suggest that bullying may also predict later involvement in a gang. When asked if they were ever bullied in school, 36% of the males and 46% of the females reported that they had "been bullied." When asked about their own bullying behavior, there was no significant difference between male and female gang members, but twice as many (62%) gang involved females answered affirmatively to the question "did you ever bully someone in school?" compared to non-gang females (30%), a statistically significant difference (Chi-square=98.1, p<.001). These findings affirm that gang involved males and females share some common experiences and behaviors, and for some behaviors, gang involved females have more in common with the gang involved males than they do with other females.

Use of Force, Making Demands, Risk-taking

Consistent with bullying, male and female gang members are also more likely to use force to get what they want. In response to the statement, "I always get what I want even if I have to take it from someone," three times as many (27%) female gang members reported that they always or usually get what they want compared to female non-gang members (6%). In contrast, twice as many (52%) female non- gang members responded "never" to the statement, compared to 20% of the gang members. These differences were statistically significant (Chi-square=152.9, p<.001). More gang girls (44%) responded that "always" or "usually," "it is all right to demand that my needs be met," compared to non-gang members (31%), a significant difference (Chi-square=26.7, p<.001). In addition, nearly twice as many gang versus non-gang members (15% vs. 8%) answered "never" to the statement, "I am careful to avoid activities in which I may be injured."

When asked to describe the difference between male and female adolescents, probation staff at the Los Padrinos Juvenile Hall reported that the girls are much more difficult to deal with. In the example that follows, the difference is made clear. When breaking up a fight between two male detainees, the probation staff may have some difficulty but will succeed in stopping the fight. When female detainees are involved in a fight, however, the probation officer is more likely to be attacked by the two females, who turn their energy toward the probation staff instead of each other. Male juveniles threaten each other before physical contact. Female detainees, knowing probation protocols, will not immediately get into an altercation while probation staff is nearby. They will, instead, make only eye contact, wait for an opportunity, and then quickly start fighting. The enemy is not surprised and is just as ready to "get down" as the girl who initiated the fight. A probation staff member will quickly break up fights, but not before a few punches have been thrown. Although most probation staff members working in the female living units are women, at least one male seems to always be present.

Because of the high level of violence in the lives of adolescents, protection may be a factor in their decision to join a gang. They may be seeking protection from further victimization, or they may be seeking protection in numbers for their own violent actions. When asked "how important was seeking protection in your decision to join a gang," 62% of the female gang members reported that seeking protection was either "important" or "very important," compared to 40% for male gang members (Knox et al., 1997). This difference between males and females was statistically significant (Chi-square=61.5, p<.001).

Gang Crime and Legal Charges

The Knox et al. (1997) survey included some questions designed to measure the respondents' perceptions of the effectiveness of harsher legal penalties imposed on violent juvenile offenders and gang related crimes. More gang involved females than non-gang members (53% vs. 39%) reported that if juveniles were tried as adults it would "not" stop them from committing a violent crime. The difference between the responses of the two groups was statistically significant (Chi-square=18.1, p<.001). Similarly, when asked if gangs were investigated and prosecuted as organized crime groups, would it put some gangs out of business, nearly twice as many (66%) female gang members responded "no" as opposed to non-gang members (34%), also a significant difference (Chi-square=88.5, p<.001).

Similarities Between Female Gang and Non-Gang Members

Although the focus in the paper so far has been on the differences between female gang and non-gang members, they share some similarities as well. Following are some of the items on the survey conducted by Knox et al. (1997) where there were no significant differences between female gang and non-gang members, with a specific focus in the areas of beliefs and attitudes, and behavior and background Factors.

Beliefs and Attitudes

Several variables measuring beliefs and attitudes were not significant in the tests comparing female non-gang members with female gang members. Gang membership made no difference in their beliefs about whether they would find a good job and eventually be able to support a family, or whether they felt that they were a part of the legitimate opportunities in their city or town or cut out of good possibilities (i.e., the underclass question). There was no difference in their beliefs about whether bullying in school can lead to gangbanging or whether they thought that early intervention in the 3rd, 4th, and 5th grade could help discourage children from joining gangs. They had similar responses as to whether they thought most gang members got arrested for crimes they committed for their gang or for crimes they committed for themselves.

Behavior and Experiential Background Factors

Similarly, several variables measuring behavioral and experiential or background factors were not significant in comparing female gang members with female non-gang members. Gang membership seemed to make no difference as to whether they were ever "bullied" by anyone in school or whether they were ever forced to have sex that they did not want to have. The girls were not significantly different in terms of whether or not in their conversations with parents, the parent(s) often showed favorable attitudes toward drugs, crime, and violence. They also similarly reported as to whether their school took it seriously when they got involved in drugs, guns, and gangs. Gang and non-gang females were no different in terms of whether or not their parent (s) took time to come and meet their teachers when they were in school or whether or not the parent (s) were physically violent in the home.

Similarities Between Male and Female Gang Members

While the earlier sections have focused primarily on comparisons between female gang and non-gang members, this section compares male and female gang members. In most areas, male and female gang members have more in common than not. Three particular areas will be discussed: beliefs and attitudes, behavior and background factors, and gang life variables. All of the information in this section is from the Project GANGFACT study (Knox et al., 1997).

Beliefs and Attitudes

There were many items where there was no statistically significant difference between male and female gang members, indicating that they shared similar beliefs and attitudes. Both males and females were unsure about whether they would be able to find a good job and eventually support a family. They were also more likely than their non-gang peers to feel that "I am not a part of legitimate opportunities in my city or town and am cut out of good possibilities" (i.e., the belief about being a part of the underclass). They tended to be more likely to support the notion that "I get what I want even if I have to take it from someone." There was no difference in their belief as to whether bullying in school can lead to gangbanging. They tended to agree that it is "all right to demand that my needs be met." Males and females tended to agree as to the degree of difficulty since March of 1994 to buy illegal guns. They agreed as to whether shooting at a police officer would bring heat on their gang or whether it would bring them status and reputation.

On a more personal note, there were no significant differences between male and female gang members in regard to whether any of their parents had ever served time in prison or whether their parents(s) were physically violent in their homes. They were also similar in terms of whether their parent(s) knew where they were and whom they were with.

Behavior and Background Factors

There was no significant difference between male and female gang members in terms of their bullying behavior at school. They were less likely to attend church than their non-gang peers. Males and females were similar in their level of risk-taking behavior, even if they might be injured. There were no significant differences in terms of their involvement in organized drug dealing, or more specifically, whether they had ever sold crack cocaine. They were less likely to have completed high school or obtained their GED.

There were also similarities between male and female gang members while they were in a correctional facility. They tended to have more disciplinary reports than non-gang members. They were more likely to have started a fight or attacked someone and more likely to have carried a homemade weapon (knife, etc.) while in custody. They were more likely to have threatened a facility staff member or officer, and they were more likely to have tried to smuggle illegal drugs into the facility.

Gang Life Variables

There were also items specifically relating to gang life and gang activities where male and female gang members responded similarly. They were less likely to think gangs could be put out of business if they were investigated and prosecuted like organized crime groups. They were more likely than their non-gang peers to have many close friends and associates that were also gang members. Males and females were similar in terms of how many had ever attempted to quit the gang. They were also similar in regard to whether or not their gang has written rules for its members, whether or not their gang held regular weekly meetings, whether or not their gang required its members to pay regular weekly dues, and whether or not their gang had older adult leaders who had been in the gang for many years. There were no significant differences in the percentages of male and female gang members who agreed that they had ever committed a crime for financial gain with their gang, or whether the chance to make money was important in their decision to join a gang.

Most gang members, males and females, would quit the gang if they had a true "second chance" to start their lives over, but over one-third think they would have still joined a gang even if there had been youth activities available to them (for example: sports, music, art, drama, YMCA, Boys' Club, church activities, etc.). They reported similar levels of racial/ethnic homogeneity/heterogeneity in their gang membership. There were no significant differences as to whether their gang had ever sold crack cocaine. Males and females were similar in terms of whether or not their parents knew they were gang members. They were similar in reporting whether or not their gang had established any relationship with real organized crime groups. Most male and female gang members think their gang has kept the promise(s) it made to them when they first joined. More than half report that the gangs inside correctional institutions are basically the same gangs that exist on the street, and less than half think they will ever be the top leader of their gang.

Males and females responded similarly as to whether gang membership had affected their religious beliefs in any way and whether or not they felt that the gang they belonged to was aiding their race or ethnic group to overcome society's prejudices. They responded similarly as to whether or not anyone in their gang (i.e., leaders, etc.) had ever told them to perform an act that they felt was wrong. Few indicated that either their father or mother had encouraged them to join a gang, and about half thought their parents would be embarrassed to learn they were in a gang. Over half said they joined a gang because they knew someone that was a member of a gang (for instance a friend, a brother, or an uncle) and that they thought they could quit the gang if they wanted to. The majority felt protected and loved by being in a gang.

Both male and female gang members gave similar responses as to whether or not they believe that in their neighborhood gang fighting was normal behavior and whether or not they felt that their school did not take it too seriously when they got involved in drugs, guns, and gangs. They were similar as to whether or not they knew of any members of the law enforcement community who were active gang members. They were similar in their thinking about whether or not early intervention in the 3rd, 4th, and 5th grade could help discourage children from joining gangs.

Within correctional facilities, male and female gang members gave similar responses as to whether gangs use religion as a front in order to conduct gang business in the institutions, and whether or not gangs seek to influence staff members to bring in drugs/contraband. Their responses were similar as to whether they had ever used legal letters to communicate with fellow gang members. Only about a third of all gang members, males and females, think that a zero tolerance approach to gang activity within a correctional facility affects gang recruitment, and about two-thirds report that there is a connection between adult prison gangs and juvenile institutional gangs.

Differences Between Male and Female Gang Members

There were several items, however, where female gang members were significantly different from their male counterparts. These include the following:

• More females were bullied in school;
• Fewer females thought gang members got arrested for crimes committed for themselves;
• Far more females had been forced to have sex they did not want to have;
• Females were more likely to live in single parent father-headed households;
• Fewer females had fired a gun at a police officer;
• More females thought trying juveniles as adults would deter juveniles from violent crime;
• More females said they did not believe in God;
• More females said they were on Satan's side;
• More females were involved in organized drug dealing for their gang vs. themselves;
• Fewer females had ever held rank in the gang;
• More females said their gang had a special language code;
• Females were more likely to do what the gang expected than whatever they wanted;
• More females joined the gang for protection;
• Fewer females asked to join the gang (they were more likely to be recruited);
• More females feel some outside person/organization controls the gang;
• Fewer females joined the gang in a correctional institution;
• More females said there were female leaders in their gang;
• More females had made "911" calls in connection with gang activities;
• More females had met face-to-face with the top leader of the gang;

• More females got their gang nickname before being locked up;
• Fewer females had parents with favorable attitudes toward drugs/crime/violence;
• Fewer females had been in a physical fight while in the correctional facility;
• Fewer females had fought with rival gang members in the correctional facility; and
• More females had known males in their gang who forced females to have sex.

Summary

Much current research focuses on the participation of girls in gangs within the context of a shift in juvenile female offender behavior toward increased violence. While studies confirm that girls today do commit a wider range of delinquent behavior than ordinarily believed, research also documents that girls have long been in gangs, and their participation in these gangs is heavily influenced by their gender. "While female gang members may engage in violent activities, the need for surrogate families, physical safety, companionship, and sometimes financial or other assistance is more critical to them" (OJJDP, 1997). In the Project GANGFACT study (Knox et al., 1997), the largest difference between male and female gang members was represented by the question, "were you ever forced to have sex that you did not want to have?" Fifteen percent of the males answered in the affirmative, while an astonishing 57.2% of the females responded the same. Thus, female gang members often come to the gang from a background of victimization and trauma. Female juvenile delinquents, including those in gangs often use alcohol and drugs to self-medicate in order to deal with powerful negative emotions and a negative environment. Durant et al. (1995) found that for gangs in general, drug and alcohol use, fighting, and gang membership were related. Feelings of anger and fear are common. Also, similar to males, gang involvement and the negative excitement that goes with gang membership can be addictive and become a way of life.

Apparently, the abuse and pain suffered in the family of origin are greater than that initially conferred by the gang. The young women may try to recreate the family they would rather have been born into in the gang. Unfortunately, gang membership and the new "family" are a return to that which is comfortable -- dysfunctional behavior carried out by a different set of "parents" and "siblings." This is clearly illustrated in the way that teenage females call the older female members "mom." Although acknowledging that their "gang mom" is not their real mother, females have reported that they feel more love and support from these surrogate parents. The "gang mom" is watchful over her "daughters" and will punish them if they have not completed their assigned "tasks." These "gang moms" may be second or third generation gang members, having at one time themselves been one of the younger members. As they are now able to provide support to their younger proteges, they feel that the responsibility for this guidance lies in their hands. The female adolescents' biological parents may be deceased, incarcerated, or just missing from their lives. The biological mother may also be unavailable, either physically or emotionally to provide the nurturing and support that the young women need. By recreating the dysfunctional family within a gang environment, the seriousness of the situation may not be recognized until it is too late. The biological parent may eventually become available and encourage the adolescent to leave the gang. Often, though, the parent him/herself may not have the resources to persist with that transition; or sometimes, in spite of all the hard work and dedication of the parent who tries to be responsible, the child may prefer to maintain her gang affiliation and remain with her gang family. Is it not human nature to stay with that which is familiar and comfortable?

As if a character in a comic book, the female may be thought of as just a mild mannered sidekick, like Robin to Batman. Trends are rapidly changing, however. The strong female delinquent can actually function quite independently. On the streets, she may demand respect, be seen as an equal and dealt with as another male. As shown in the data from Project GANGFACT, in many ways female gang members do not behave very differently than their male counterparts. One thing that has eliminated the inequality between males and females is the firearm. Interestingly, it is the males who have taught the females the efficiency of firearms; some have gone so far as to provide firearms and limited training to females. Along with increasing her parity with male gang members, though, her increased involvement in criminal activities also increases the likelihood of her arrest.

Historically, the criminal justice system has been dominated by male offenders -- both adult and juvenile. It is no wonder that the concerns and needs of young women remain overlooked. In the future, research should be conducted to determine their most essential needs. That information should then be used to develop programs specifically designed to meet the needs of female offenders. Females in correctional programs should be able to discuss their most difficult life situations and decide which ones they are ready to address. Needs assessments should also be conducted to identify and address gaps in service delivery. Participants' advice, knowledge, and suggestions must be sought throughout program development and implementation, and not only once. Areas to be discussed and addressed with the girls could be communication styles, anger, aggression, motherhood, female gang involvement, and dealing with death and loss. Their past victimization needs to be addressed, as well as any substance abuse problems they might have, and this needs to be done in a supportive environment. Further, currently existing programs proven to be successful should be enhanced and expanded.

One of the barriers to improving services for incarcerated female adolescents is that few correctional employees are interested in working with them. From the personal experience of this author, female detainees are described as over-emotional, loud, rude, and crazy. Staff maintain that it is difficult, if not impossible, to maintain an environment conducive to learning. On the other hand, many of these young women are creative, out-spoken, confident, and possess a strong sense of fairness. They are assertive, loyal, and "ready for action". If they disagree with someone, they are generally able to stand up and defend their side. Their assertion regarding the information they deem incorrect will be debated until the other person has backed down or agreed with them. Perhaps this has been caused by not having enough positive support when they were younger, or perhaps it is just one of the ways adolescent females attempt to be visible and "heard." Most are very open about admitting gang affiliation, naming names, and describing their daily activities. Often, the real names of their "gang associates" are not known; that could be the explanation for the openness to discuss their homeboys.

Primary and Secondary Prevention Strategies

In addition to research in the area of prevention, educators, health practitioners, mental health providers and social service workers have suggested ideas to strengthen social, personal, and environmental factors in an effort to deter young people from engaging in delinquent behavior, including joining gangs. In addition to delivering effective interventions, it is equally important for those working with gang prevention to communicate directly and clearly, be committed, optimistic and involved, and show a concerned, humorous, caring, and non-judgmental attitude. Following are some suggested interventions for dealing with particular problems that may be presented by young people, males and females, who are involved with the juvenile justice system.

Indicators and Methods

Education
Determine Learning Style Preference, Use of Tutoring, Place Youth into an Environment That They Find Comfortable and Challenging.

Job Skills
Determine Level of Skills and Abilities. Provide Training in Careers Where Jobs Are Interesting to Youth and Available.

Stress, Tension, & Anxiety
Assessment and Counseling, Exercise Groups, Teach Meditation and Relaxation Exercises.

Relationships
Attend Workshops and Support Groups to Teach the Dynamics of Healthy Relationships.

Co-dependency
Attend 12-step Co-dependents Meetings, Mentors, Assertiveness Training, Assistance with New Living Arrangements.

Family Members who misuse drugs and/or alcohol.
Attend 12-Step Al-Anon & Nar-Anon Meetings, Group Support, Teams, Individual Counseling.

Communication Skills Building
Use Learning Preferences to Train Teachers, Teachers Aides and Staff. Alter Learning Environment So That it Is More Conducive to a Supportive Learning Environment.

Domestic Violence
Referral, Support Groups, Adequate Number of and Access to Safe Houses, Counseling.

Parenting
Volunteer Workshops, Classes, and Support Groups. Avoid Conservative Classroom Style and Use Culturally Competent, Experienced Parents as Facilitators.

Drug & Alcohol Misuse
12-Step Meetings of Alcoholics Anonymous, Narcotics Anonymous, Crystal Meth Anonymous, Marijuana Anonymous, Cocaine Anonymous, etc.

Community
Community Coalition Building.

Lack of Resources
Create and Maintain Up-dated Resource Guide with Toll Free Numbers to Youth Serving Agencies, Such as Mentoring Hotline: (800) 55-YOUTH.

REFERENCES

Anderson, N.L. 1994. Resolutions and risk-taking in juvenile detention. *Clinical Nursing Research,* 3(4): 297-315.

Ash, P., Kellermann, A.L., Fugua-Whitley, D., Johnson, A. 1996. Gun acquisition and use by juvenile offenders. *Journal of the American Medical Association,* 275 (22): 1754-8.

Brown, R. 1993. Girls in the juvenile justice system (cassette recording). Florida: Meeting of the National Commission on Correctional Health Care.

Bishop, D.M. & Frazier, C.E. 1991. Transfer of juveniles to criminal court: A case study of prosecutorial waiver. *Notre Dame Journal of Law, Ethics and Public Policy,* 5(2):281-302.

Bureau of Justice Statistics. 1996. *National criminal justice statistics.* Washington, D.C.: U. S. Department of Justice, Office of Justice Programs, Bureau of Justice Statistics.

Casper, R.C., Belanoff, J., and Offer, D. 1996. Gender differences, but no racial group differences, in self-reported psychiatric symptoms in adolescents. *Journal of the American Academy of Child and Adolescent Psychiatry,* 35(4): 500-508.

Chang, J. 1996. A comparative study of female gang and non-gang members in Chicago. *Journal of Gang Research,* 2(6).

Chesney-Lind, M., and Shelden, R.G. 1998. *Girls, delinquency, and juvenile justice.* Belmont, CA: West/Wadsworth.

Christopher, W., Chair, Independent Commission on the Los Angeles Police Department. 1991. *Report of the independent commission on the Los Angeles Police Department: Summary Report.* Los Angeles: Los Angeles Police Department.

Donziger, S.R., (Ed.). 1996. *The real war on crime: A report of the National Criminal Justice Commission.* New York: HarperCollins Publishers, Inc.

Durant, R.H., Getts, A.G., Cadenhead, C., and Woods, E.R. 1995. The association between weapon carrying and the use of violence among adolescents living in and around public housing. *Journal of Adolescent Health, 17*(6): 376-80.

electric.ss.uci.edu/~rickg/gangs2000/executive.html.

Gilliard, D.K. & Allen J. Beck. 1997. *Prison and jail inmates at midyear 1996.* Washington, D.C.: U.S. Department of Justice, Office of Justice Programs, Bureau of Justice Statistics.

Girls, Inc. 1996. *Prevention and parity: Girls in juvenile justice.* Washington, D.C.: Office Of Juvenile Justice and Delinquency Prevention.

Knox, G. W. and the 28 co-principal investigators of Project GANGFACT. 1997. *The facts about gang life in America today: A national study of over 4,000 gang members.* Chicago: National Gang Crime Research Center.

Lewandowski, L.M. and Westman, A.S. 1996. Social support desired vs received by high school students in or not in a delinquency prevention program. *Psychological Reports,* 78(6): 111-114.

Lie, N. and Wagner, E.E. 1996. Prediction of criminal behavior in young Swedish women using a group administration of the Hand Test. *Perceptual & Motor Skills*, 82 (3 Pt 1): 975-978.

Males, M. 1996. *The scapegoat generation: America's war on adolescents*. Common Courage Press.

Molidor, C.E. 1996. Female gang members: A profile of aggression, and victimization. *Social Work*, 41 (3): 251-257.

Office of Juvenile Justice and Delinquency Prevention. 1997. *Training and technical assistance program to promote gender-specific programming for female juvenile offenders and at-risk girls.* Washington, D.C.: U.S. Department of Justice, Office of Justice Programs, Office of Juvenile Justice and Delinquency Prevention.

Romero, D.J. 1998 (January 1). Criminalization of teen culture booms. *The Los Angeles Times*, E6.

Snell, T. L. and Morton, D. C. 1994. *Women in prison: Survey of state prison inmates, 1991.* Washington, D.C.: U. S. Department of Justice, Office of Justice Programs, Bureau of Justice Statistics.

Snyder, H.K. 1999. *Juvenile arrests 1998.* Bulletin. Washington, D.C.: U.S. Department of Justice, Office of Justice Programs, Office of Juvenile Justice and Delinquency Prevention.

Timmons-Mitchell, J., Brown, C., Schulz, S.C., Webster, S.E., Underwood, L.A., and Semple, W.E. 1997. Comparing the mental health needs of female and male incarcerated juvenile delinquents. *Behavioral Sciences & the Law*, 15 (2): 195-202.

CHAPTER SEVEN

INSIDE GANG SOCIETY:
HOW GANG MEMBERS IMITATE LEGITIMATE SOCIAL
FORMS

Alice P. Franklin Elder, Ph.D.
Ohio Youth Services

The word gang has become a synonym for any youth violence regardless of whether the violent act is committed by a specific individual or a collective of individuals. Many also perceive the gang as devoting its full-time energies to committing violent and illegal acts. Research shows, however, that gangs participate in both illegal and legal enterprises (Jankowski, 1991).

It is because violent crimes pose such a threat to the safety and security of American communities that the public's emotional outcry has demanded both a cessation of individual crimes and an immediate solution to the overall crime problem. While these responses are understandable, they are void of the type of objective reasoning and facts that are necessary for finding effective prevention and intervention solutions to the gang problem.

This paper offers insights on how our current knowledge of gangs and organizational behavior can help us in understanding and preventing the development and persistence of gangs (including how to create constructive alternatives for at - risk youth who may be prone to participate in gangs). The purpose of this paper is twofold: **One** to further explicate the existence and role of the gang organization in order to isolate patterned behavior relative to its structure, operational process, environmental relations, etc.; and **Two**, to better understand the gang as a business enterprise where gang members seek to achieve economic goals through the gang organization.

At a minimum, the organizational approach to gang study calls for rethinking and re-examining the gang violence issue. A beginning is to recognize that violent acts can be caused by specific individuals acting autonomously as well by a group of individuals acting in concert as a gang organization. **It is the gang organization, itself, and its characteristics that are the focus of this paper.** The gang is viewed as an organized association consisting primarily of juvenile offenders. Within this context, the gang is more specifically defined as an illegal business organization consisting primarily of low income juvenile offenders who make economic and social adaptations to society through the benefits they gain from the collective illegal and legal activities of their gang membership (Padilla, 1992).[1]

Society's failure to make a distinction in its media reporting and its corrective responses between individual acts of violence and violence committed by an organized group continues to direct prevention and intervention efforts away from meaningful strategies where solutions could be found. For example, if most community violence is caused and perpetuated by individuals merely acting on their own impulses, then successful retribution and deterrence should have been achieved already through incarcerative means alone. This has not occurred. Violence has increased and the gang has persisted. Given these circumstances, there is good reason to call into question the public's emotional assumption that it does not matter whether it is individual or group violence - violence is violence. Theoretically, however, individual and collective violence are not the same.

From a social science and policy stance, it is important to distinguish the emotional and physical consequences of violence for a victim implemented by an autonomous individual from the sociological and physical consequences of violence implemented by an an organized group. Sociologically, collective violence is significantly more threatening to a community than individual violence not only because of the sheer number of persons involved in committing the act, but also because of the consensus impact underlying its implementation. Secondly, collective acts of violence are more likely to persist over time when they are supported and sanctioned by an organized effort, i.e., an organized gang. This second observation is particularly important as we consider appropriate designs for specific types of prevention and intervention strategies (Jankowski, 1991).[2] Consequently, in addition to recognizing the gang as an organization that provides economic supports to its members, this paper also examines the etiology of the gang's persistence (stability) and how the organizational perspective can be effectively used as a theoretical basis for explaining and controlling this phenomenon.

Violence is what society fears and hates the most; yet, a preoccupation with and sensationalizing of individual acts of violence inhibits and/or prevents efforts to better understand violence as the instrument or means of gangs and not just the gang's end (as it is often perceived by the public). The end results for those who are involved in collective gang activity is gang organizational survival--not just violence itself. The gang organization, like other organizations, gives a high priority to its own survival (Jankowski,1991; Knox, 1994).

Specifically, this paper argues that the organizational process and the structure of the gang organization are similar to many other legitimate organizations whose goals are profit and survival. To understand the gang organization, it is important to apply our knowledge of organizations in general to this specific entity. Additionally, activities of the gang organization are not restricted to just illegal pursuits, but include both illegal and legal acts. Jankowski's (1991) research supports this emphasis that gangs are not merely a group of delinquents preoccupied with reeking violence on individuals and communities, but rather organized collectives that seek profit and participation through all illegal and legal means available. Therefore, viewing the gang as an alternative business enterprise that has a primary mission of profit appears to be an effective way to understand why juveniles participate, and why the gang has persisted over time.

Again, violence is an instrument used by gangs to assist its efforts in amassing profits and participating in society (Jankowski, 1991). As a business organization, the gang can be expected to imitate and apply forms and processes that are deemed effective in legitimate societal organizations for structuring themselves to successfully attain their economic goals (Thompson, 1967). Society's failure to fully appreciate the entrepreneurial skills of gang members and their economic goals, and to translate available knowledge of gang organizations into effective prevention and intervention strategies appears to be hindered by particular views that society has of gang members.

Jankowski (1991) says the problem possibly stems from the fact that because gang members are often involved in activities that are labeled illegal or illegitimate, there is a reluctance on society's part to view them (gang members, particularly gang leaders) as being similar in ability and intelligence to the "law-abiding best and brightest" in legitimate society. However, the persistence and stability of some gangs over time strongly suggests that creative leadership is also present among this group. Moreover, other studies suggest a patterning of the organizational behavior itself that makes important aspects of the gang operation, form, and structure quite effective in achieving its goals (albeit goals that society deems illegal due to the means used to achieve them).

A first step in gaining a broader understanding of why juveniles participate in gangs, and why gang organizations evolve to support and reinforce this participation, can be found in examining the gang's belief system and gang's perspective of the wider society. Jankowski (1991) found in his research that the patterning of the gang behavior he studied was associated with the gang's adoption of a foundational belief system about society and how gang members felt they had to relate to society. According to Thompson's (1967) perspective on organizational behavior, a belief system creates a collective identity that reinforces a certain type of conduct among organizational members. Such a belief system has the potential to counter society's view of the gang for gang members, as well as undermine society's legitimate belief system.

Gang Members' Perspective on Society

Padilla (1992) and Jankowski (1991) summarize gang members' perspective of society. Padilla (1992) suggests that society's economically poor (primarily Latino and African-American) young people have . . . "lost faith in the capacity of the society to work on their behalf . . . and deliver the kinds of emotional support and material goods the larger society promises but does not make available to youngsters like themselves . . . they have responded to their conditions by developing or joining gangs . . ." (p. 2). Gang members in Padilla's research believed that" . . . the gang represents the only course of action still available to them and with which they can challenge existing constraints in and domination by mainstream society . . . These young people joined the gang in pursuit of economic advantages . . . There is nothing exaggerated, fanciful, or theoretical in the pronouncement that the gang provides a mechanism of survival for its members . . ." (p. 5).

Nearly all the gangs studied by Jankowski (1991) believed that their ethnic group had been denied access to conventional opportunities that would allow them to live more comfortable lives. The youth with low formal education, income, and status did not feel they had access to legitimate opportunities for upward mobility. For these youth, crime and the gang were viewed as an alternative adaptation that they believed was necessary to accommodate their circumstances. Specifically, they believed that the people who are successful are successful because they are competitive and prey on others less able to defend themselves. They also use illegal methods to get what they want. In turn, they (gang members) saw that the only way for them to survive was to organize themselves.

Padilla (1992) also suggests that when members first join a gang they believe it will take care of all their needs. The gang represents hope and a viable means by which youth can gain self-respect, protection, employment opportunities, etc. However, as a business organization, gangs are profit-oriented, and because profit has a priority over most other considerations, gang organizations are not able to always live up to providing the ideal supports that were advocated during recruitment. For example, in Padilla's research there were gang members who had spent years working as street-level dealers before they came to recognize that their labor was consistently taken advantage of and exploited. They believed their work had primarily benefited the gang's main heads, or top-level distributors and suppliers. As street-level dealers, they ultimately had to come to terms with their permanent position as wage earners. "Against perceived conditions of gang domination and inequality, several members decided to cut their ties with the gang and return to the very same world they had earlier opposed." (p. 2).

Society also has its own perception of gang members. Society believes gang members to be individuals of the lowest of the lower class, with low intelligence, psychological disorders (like sadism) and no initiative to work for a living (Jankowski, 1991). However, research conducted by both Jankowski and Padilla offers findings to challenge the accuracy of this perception. According to Jankowski (1991), while there is a " . . . great range of individuals in gangs, . . .the vast majority of gang members are quite energetic and are eager to acquire many of the same things that most members of American society want: money, material possessions, power and prestige . . . Because they want the "good life," they energetically seek entrepreneurial opportunities that might lead them to it . . . thus a given gang member's display of aggressive traits or his involvement in violent exchange is not necessarily pathological; rather it is appropriate behavior in an environment whose socio-economic conditions are pathological." (p. 312).

In Padilla's (1992) research, the decision by gang members to participate in the gang organization was "informed not only by their assessments of the lack of available opportunities in the regular economy but also by their high level of aspirations . . . Rather than the gang arising as a deliberate violation of middle class aspirations, the gang represents a counter organization, a response geared to fulfilling the standards of the larger society . . ." (p. 103). In effect, what these youngsters did was reconstruct the "criminal" gang into an income generating business operation - an alternative form of employment with which they could hope to "make it" in U.S. society.

An understanding of youth participation in gangs and why gang organizations exist as adaptive alternatives can be analogized to how African Americans were forced to adopt the following institutional alternatives in order to participate in society:

1. African American colleges and universities were established.
2. African American sororities and fraternities were established.
3. African American churches were established.

These institutions were alternative adaptations created by individuals living in a society where access to full participation in traditionally white universities, churches, colleges, and the general society at large was automatically denied persons of the Black race.

Placing the belief system of the gang in theoretical perspective helps to explain the gang's function as a viable illegitimate economic alternative to conventional business. An examination of the gang's belief system and the perspective of the gang demonstrates how the foundation is laid for the organization to emerge. Assuming the gang requires, as do other organizations, a belief system, a patterned structure, and specific resources to develop and become effective, we may then use our current knowledge of organizational behavior to manipulate a given structure and/or the behavior of gang members, thereby making it:

1. Difficult for a gang to move from a loose knit group to an organized association; and

2. Difficult for the gang organization to survive over time by altering its external relations and its access to needed internal and external resources.

This author will now examine the gang as an organizational entity and describe the extent to which it also mirrors other legitimate organizations in society. National needs assessments conducted by Knox et al. (1995; 1997) support earlier research which found that gangs represented distinct organizational entities. Also, many of these gangs appear to have a variable complexity in internal structure and established external relations. Additionally, these gang organizations tend to perform certain maintenance requirements and activities that are geared to ensure operational success.

The national surveys conducted by Knox et al. (1995, 1997) contained approximately 2,000 gang members from eight states in the first and approximately 4,000 gang members in 17 states in the second (included current and/or past gang membership). From these data, gang organizations were profiled on the characteristics of their form, structure and maintenance requirements (see Table 1). Approximately 72 percent of those surveyed (71.9%, N=1,389) in the early study and 65 percent of those surveyed (65.0%, N=2,627) more recently stated they were currently members of a gang. Also in the earlier study, either in addition to or in lieu of current gang membership, 69 percent of the respondents stated that they were associated with a gang organization. The gang's existence as an organizationally sophisticated and complex entity was substantiated in this national research on gang member participation. Table 2 summarizes the **organizational characteristics** shared between the gang organization and those described for legitimate organizations by Thompson (1967) and Etizoni (1964).

Tables 1 and 2 describe several features associated with the gang organizations studied that mirror characteristics of legitimate societal organizations. **Shared characteristics included**: decision/management/leadership structure, core membership, membership recruitment practice, membership dues requirement, defined performance expectations, tenured membership, scheduled meetings, financial base, communication system ideological belief system, sanctioning and control system, legal resources, community relations and societal linkages, role stratification, and organizational complexities. The findings below elaborate the decision/management/leadership structure and the internal maintenance structure.

A vertical hierarchy characterizes the gang's overall management/leadership structure. To measure this feature, the first national survey conducted by Knox et al. (1995) asked whether the respondent felt it was true or false that "In my gang, the things the gang does are approved by a higher up leader." Over 60 percent (63.3%) stated this was true. Jankowski (1991) states that "In order to function as efficiently as possible, gangs establish organizations with particular structures . . ." The first part of this structure addresses formal leadership whereby ". . . leadership categories are labeled and assigned a degree of authority . . ." (p. 78).

Table 1
A Summary of Key Organizational Characteristics of Gangs

Gang Organization Form/Structure
1. Decision/Management/Leadership Structure
        Hierarchical
Gang Organizational Maintenance Requirements and Activities
2. Core Identifiable Membership
3. Membership Recruitment Practice
4. Membership Dues Requirement
5. Member Participation in Illegal Activities
6. Tenured/Long Term Membership
7. Regularly Scheduled Meeting Practice
8. Established Financial Base Revenue
9. Communication System (Special Language/Linguistic System) in
        Operation
10. Ideology (Belief) System in Operation
11. Social Control and Sanction Process in Operation
12. Legal Resources Recruited/Maintained for:
        Private Attorney
        Legal Defense Fund
        Assistance to gang members and/or their families
13. Community Relations and Societal Linkages Sought (e.g., Positive
        Media Coverage)
14. Roles Stratification

    The gang's internal maintenance structure included these requirements: core membership, new member recruitment, defined performance expectations (e.g., there is an expectation that members will participate in illegal activities), tenured affiliation, regularly scheduled meetings, a financial base, a communication system, a control and sanctioning system, legal resources, a role stratification structure, an ideological system, and written rules. Knox et al. (1995) found that a little over 50 percent (50.7%, N=875) of the gang members surveyed stated their gang had a core membership, and a list with the names of these members was also kept. Approximately 70 percent (70.9%, N=1,266) had recruited someone else into the gang. It also appears that for the majority of the gang respondents in this study, new applicants to their gang were not automatically accepted for membership, since approximately 66 percent stated that new applicant membership had been turned down. This finding support Jankowski's (1991) research which showed that ". . .The gang deliberately does not have an open-door policy on membership. It cannot allow every individual who wants to be a member to join. Decisions concerning membership are dependent on assessments of its needs by the organization . . ." (p. 30).
    Although specific expectations for organizational members will differ, gang organizations,like non-gang organizations have defined performance

expectations for their members. Knox et al. (1995) found that a little over 40 percent (40.9%, N=728) of the members stated that their gang required them to maintain tenured affiliation with the gang. In essence, they could not just resign from the gang whenever they felt like it. Approximately 40 percent (39.2%, N=688) stated that they were required to participate in illegal activities, and many (60.7%, N=1,111) had committed a crime for financial gain with their gang. That same question was asked in the more recent survey as well (Knox et al., 1997), and about the same percent of respondents (58.5%, N=2.344) said they had committed a crime for financial gain with their gang.

Table 2
Shared Characteristics Between Gang Organizations and Legitimate Societal Organizations.

Shared Characteristics	Type of Organization	
	Gang	Legitimate
Core Membership	Yes	Yes
Membership Recruitment	Yes	Yes
Membership Dues	Yes	Yes*
Participation in Illegal Activities	Yes	No**
Tenured/Long Term Membership	Yes	Yes
Regularly Scheduled Meetings	Yes	Yes
Available Treasury	Yes	Yes
Communication Sysem (i.e., special language, linguistic system)	Yes	Yes
Ideology (Belief) System	Yes	Yes
Social Control and Sanctioning Process	Yes	Yes
Legal Resources	Yes	Yes
Community Relations and Societal Linkages	Yes	Yes

* Sometimes
** Not sanctioned by legitimate organizations

Like other organizations, gangs must maintain certain economic, political, and social functions and must recruit resources to support these operations. Findings from the study conducted by Knox et al. (1995) indicate that approximately 60 percent (59.8%, N = 1,052) of gang members surveyed said that their gang maintained a treasury. Over 70 percent (73.9%, N = 1,334) of gang members indicated that their gang provided money to needy members in or out of jail or prison. Over a third (35.6%, N = 625) stated that their gang had a private attorney that was used to defend the gang in criminal matters. Additionally, over 40 percent (43.7%, N = 778) stated that their gang kept an account that was only used to pay for legal defense.

A control and sanctioning system operated in gang organizations studied to ensure that performance expectations were approximately carried out. The Knox et al. (1995) study found that approximately 44 percent (44.3%, N = 799) of gang members said they had been personally subjected to an internal disciplinary procedure where violence had been used against them. Approximately 66 percent (66.1%, N=1212) said that their gang had written rules. The more recent study (Knox et al., 1997) similarly found that about 68% of respondents said their gang had written rules (67.9%, N=2,711). That study also found that some 59 percent (59.3%, N=2,366) of respondents said that their gang had a special language code. These findings support other research, which shows that ". . . regardless of the type of leadership structure adopted, each of the gangs studied employed three mechanisms to create and maintain internal organizational control: formal codes, collective ideology, and social conflict" (Jankowski, 1991, p. 78).

In the earlier Knox et al. (1995) national research on gang organizations, stratification occurred mainly by age and responsibility. All of the gang members surveyed were male. The older gang members appeared to occupy the major leadership positions. Over eighty percent (84.8%, N =1,556) reported having older adults as leaders in their gang. Two - thirds (65.3%, N = 1,242) stated that they themselves had held a rank or leadership position in the gang. Only a third (34.7%, N = 661) had never held rank or any leadership position in their gang. The more recent study conducted by Knox et al. (1997) included both males and females, although the respondents, like the incarcerated population in general, were predominantly male (89%). Nevertheless, the findings were similar. Some 84 percent (84.3%, N=3,367) said they had older adult leaders in their gangs, and about 60 percent (59.8%, N=2,386) said that they had held a leadership position in the gang.

Legitimate societal organizations and gang organizations share several critical structural and process characteristics. The exception to shared characteristics is the gang's tendency to consistently require that members pay dues and participate in illegal activities. Conversely, in legitimate society a membership dues requirement will vary with the type of organization under consideration. On the other hand, no legitimate organization can legally require any of its members to participate in illegal activities, yet some individual members can and do participate autonomously in such activities. The crucial difference is that this illegal behavior is not sanctioned by the organization.

Table 3 below relates the nature of the gang organization's form and structure to levels of gang involvement (low, medium, and high). The research conducted by Knox et al. (1995) included 15 items that were used to construct a gang risk assessment continuum. The items were characteristics or behaviors common to gang members, and each respondent was given one point for each of the 15 items he answered affirmatively. Following is a list of the items included in the assessment: one or more close friends in a gang; family members in a gang; considers self an "associate" of a gang; has a gang tattoo; ever joined a gang; still active in a gang; been in a gang for five years or more; ever held rank in a gang; ever helped recruit new members into a gang; ever fired a gun at someone because they were threatening the drug business of the gang; never attempted to quit the gang; ever been a shooter in a drive-by shooting; ever fired a gun at someone in defense of the gang turf; expect to be a gang member for the next five years; and willing to die for their gang friends. Based on a respondent's cumulative score, he was then categorized according to level of gang involvement. Approximately 30 percent of the respondents had scores of zero or one, and they were considered the least level of gang risk. Respondents scoring between two and five (18.8%) were categorized as having a low level of gang involvement. Approximately 25 percent scored between six and nine, and they were categorized as having a moderate level of gang involvement. The group with the highest level of gang involvement scored between 10 and 15 on the assessment, which accounted for about 25 percent of the respondents. An analysis of the percent of respondents in each of the high, moderate and low categories that answered affirmatively to the gang structure/organizational items shows a positive relationship between organizational complexity and levels of gang participation. Juveniles with the highest level of gang involvement tended to be associated with the most sophisticated and complex gang organizational structures.[3]

Table 3
Organizational Complexity and Levels of Gang Participation

Organizational Characteristics	Levels of Gang Participation		
	Low Percent	Medium Percent	High Percent
Decision/Management/ Leadership Structure	52.7	61.3	65.6
Membership Composition, i.e. Core Membership	40.4	48.3	55.5
Membership Recruitment	58.5	72.3	84.0
Membership Dues	25.7	43.4	44.5
Formal Rules (i.e. Written Rules)	42.4	64.6	69.3
Tenured Membership	55.6	83.0	91.3
Regularly Scheduled Meetings	49.5	69.3	86.4
Treasury	33.3	58.9	68.4
Communication System (Special Language/ Linguistic System)	34.0	55.9	68.5
Social Control	25.1	42.9	51.8
Legal Resources, i.e. Private Attorney	20.3	30.5	45.9

These findings support other research that substantiated the existence of gangs as organized entities and not merely loose-knit groups (i.e., Knox 1994, Jankowski 1991, and Padilla 1992). The more sophisticated and tenured a gang is, the more closely it mirrors the theoretical and traditional models of organizational behavior and the organizational process.

In Table 4, Olsen (1968) describes several basic structural and environmental requirements associated with legitimate organizations that are necessary for them to achieve effective functioning and to remain stable over time. As can be observed, these requirements closely correspond to the characteristics of the gang organization that we previously discussed, including the requirements that there be organizational interdependence with other systems in the gang's environment. In Table 4, numbers 1 – 8, 10 - 12, and 14 - 17 address factors that focus on improving internal operations of the organization, while numbers 9 and 13 are geared to external operational improvements.

Table 4
Structural and Environmental Requirements of
Societal Organizations

1. Maintenance of the population, through either reproduction or recruitment.
2. Provision for the training and/or socialization of members of the organization.
3. Promotion of communication and interaction among members and parts of the organization.
4. Establishment of a division-of-labor through specialization of tasks, activities, duties, and responsibilities.
5. Assignment of social actors to necessary roles, or tasks, activities, duties, and responsibilities.
6. Ordering of relationships among the component parts of the organization.
7. Sharing of common social values among the adequate set of social norms and rules.
8. Establishment of a common, consistent, and adequate set of social norms and rules.
9. Procurement of necessary resources from the natural and social environment.
10. Development of methods for organizational decision-making.
11. Coordination of organizational activities so as to achieve organizational goals.
12. Provision for the allocation to members of the benefits of organizational activities.
13. Protection of the organization against external threats and stresses.
14. Control of deviant and disruptive actions by organizational members.
15. Creation of procedures for managing or resolving conflicts within the organization.
16. Promotion of organizational unity or integration.
17. Development of procedures for changing the organization.

According to Jankowski (1991), ". . . ultimately, the fate of any one gang will depend on how well it is able to recruit individuals who can help the organization; effectively manage individuals inside the organization; establish authority and become a viable and efficient economic organization; maintain good relations with its local community; and establish linkages with social institutions outside the local community by constructing mutual exchange relationships with certain individuals in them" (p. 316).

The Knox et al. (1995) national needs assessment research lends support to the above observation and other important findings about the behavior of gang organizations. Tables 1 - 4 describe the patterning in structural characteristics and in relational behavior for both legitimate organizations and gang organizations. Several of these characteristics are indicators of the gang's organizational complexity and community interdependence. Also supporting these empirical findings on how the gang organization attempts to imitate legitimate social forms are the classical works of the social theorists Olsen (1968), Thompson (1967), and March and Simon (1967). Each has emphasized the role of uncertainty and the importance of controlling uncertainty in the environment of complex organizations where goal achievement and stability are desired.

Conformance with such organizational requirements as described in Table 4 reduces and/or eliminates organizational uncertainty - one of the greatest and most fundamental concerns of any complex organization (Olsen, 1968; Thompson, 1967). Thompson (1967) states that the basic sources of uncertainty for organizations are technology (desired outcomes) and environmental (i.e., organizational relations and interdependencies with an external system or systems). According to March and Simon (1967), predictability combined with particular related structural features of organizations account for how well an organization is able to deal in a coordinated way with its environment.

An ability to identify patterned behavior in gang organizations and to profile these organizations on specific structural and relational factors contributes to a broader understanding of gangs and how loose knit groups may be prevented from evolving into organized gang structures. The nature of the gang's internal structure plays an important role in determining how the organization will function and to what extent it will be effective. But like non-gang organizations, gangs are also dependent on co-operative relations with their external environment for the recruitment of resources (Jankowski, 1991, p. 195). Externally, the importance of community relations and societal linkages with legitimate organizations and other gang groups was demonstrated in the Knox et al. (1995) research.

The media, for example, appear to play an important role in gang recruitment efforts. Also, Knox et al. (1995) found that the specific impact of the media on recruitment efforts varied with levels of gang involvement. About 44 percent (44.2%, N=852) of gang members believed that more new members tended to join the gang under conditions where intensive news coverage occurred. This finding varied with the gang member's level of participation; for example, 56 percent of the members with the lowest level of involvement (Level 1) believed this, while it was believed by 72 percent of Level 2 and 84 percent of Level 3 members.

Knox et al. (1995) also found that linkages were established with other gang groups. Some 60 percent of the gang members stated that their gang was an official branch of a larger national group. Approximately half (49.1%, N = 857) stated that their gang rose on its own locally with contact and help from gangs by the same name in another area. This type of coordination is essential for an organization to accomplish the goals that lead to its persisting overtime. A ". . .gang's success appears to be a result of four factors: control of competition, type of organizational structure, the stability of division - of - labor, and avoidance of antagonizing the community" (Jankowski, 1991, p. 126).

It appears that any organization that hopes to be effective in surviving and achieving its goals will require a particular internal structure and certain interdependent relations with external groups/organizations. Consequently, the identification of certain patterns in organizational characteristics creates promising opportunities for social science knowledge to be effectively used in the design and development of approaches to gang prevention and intervention treatment. The national research conducted by Knox et al. (1995) reinforces the importance of determining how certain structural characteristics and organizational requirements may function to aid the survival and stability of gangs. Practically, correctional policies that are merely targeted to specific individuals may not have a significant impact on gang organizations themselves, primarily because new gang members can be recruited when old ones are incarcerated, die or fall by the wayside. Only policies that can affect both the individual and the organization's ability to effectively operate can pose a serious challenge to keeping gangs from flourishing.

Continued research on gang organizations, desired outcomes sought by gangs, and the types of uncertainties associated with gang organizations and their environments is needed. The purpose of such research is to assist in engineering appropriate conditions that can lead to the demise of gangs. Building on the findings from the Knox et al. (1995) national study on how legitimate social forms are imitated, social scientists can use this knowledge to systematically manipulate the process for gang development and gang organizational stability.

Conclusion

As shown here, more recent research lends support to past findings that have described gangs as organized social entities designed to meet certain social and economic needs of participating members. The national gang research conducted by Knox et al. (1995) establishes quite definitely that gangs are more than loose knit delinquent peer groups; they are organized social entities that can have a membership tenure and stability that extends up to an average of 4.5 years.

Practically, it is important that social policy distinguishes between corrective strategies designed for individual gang members and those directed toward the gang organization itself. Since organizational behavior is sociologically different from individual behavior, prevention and intervention efforts must not be restricted solely to "treating" the individual in searching for ways to effectively impact the destruction of the gang organization and find solutions to the problem of gang violence.

A first step toward controlling the development of the gang organization and the participation of juveniles in gangs may begin with offering a counter position to the ideological socialization of the gang's belief system. Jankowski's (1991) research showed how gangs have employed ideology as an organizational resource for explaining why their members should be in the gang and solidifying the members' allegiance to the group through bonding, unity and identity. If juveniles continue to see gangs as the only alternative for adapting to their lack of economic opportunities within legitimate society and hold the belief that society does not care what happens to them, we may expect certain juveniles to continue to be especially vulnerable to the recruitment and socialization practices of gangs.

APPENDIX A

Survey Questions Re: The Gang As A Social Organization

1.   Are you currently a member of any gang group or gang organization?
2.   Do you consider yourself a current associate of any gang group or gang organization?
3.   Have you ever held rank or any leadership position in any gang?
4.   Have you ever been "violated" (received a beating) by your own gang?
5.   Does your gang have a special language code?
6.   Does your gang have written rules?
7.   Does your gang have adult leaders who have been in the gang for many years?
8.   Does your gang exist in several different geographical areas or does it exist in just one area?
9.   Does your gang provide money to needy members in or out of jail/prison?
10. Have you ever committed a crime for financial gain with your gang?
11. Does your gang have a private attorney that you use for defending your members in critical matters?
12. Does your gang keep an account that pays for only legal defense?
13. Does your gang hold regular meetings?
14. Which best describes your gang: Homegrown (emerging on its own in our city); an official branch of a larger national gang?
15. How long has your gang existed in your town?
16. Does the gang you are in have a treasury?
17. Does your gang require members to pay regular dues?
18. In your gang does a person have to participate in an illegal activity before the person can become accepted as a member of the gang?
19. Have you ever recruited anyone into the gang?
20. In my gang, members may leave the gang by resigning at any time.
21. In my gang, each member's personal life is known to other members.
22. In my gang, the things the gang does are approved by a higher up leader.
23. In my gang, no applicants for membership in the gang are turned down.
24. In my gang, the gang has meetings at regularly scheduled times.
25. In my gang, the gang keeps a list of names of the members.

END NOTES

1.   Referenced by Felix M. Padilla, <u>The Gang As An American Enterprise</u>, New Brunswick: Rutgers University Press, 1992, p.3
      Padilla's research (1989 - 1990) emphasized the business aspects of gang organizations vs their perceived occupational function. His study is based on 2nd generation Puerto Rican juveniles who belonged to a Chicago street gang that was given the fictitious name the "Diamond" gang. Gang members operate a street-level drug dealing enterprise. The gang members studied were a leading sub-group within the larger "Diamond" organization.

2.   Referenced by Martin Sanitize Jankowski (1991), p. 311; p. 314.
      ". . . gangs persist in part because the gangs themselves make concerted organizational efforts to ensure their own survival. . ." p. 311
      ". . . As an organization, the gang sees its primary concern to be organizational survival . . ." p. 314
      Jankowski's research involved a ten year study (1978 - 1989) of 37 different gangs that resided in Los Angeles, New York, and Boston cities. The study was a comparative study of different ethnic groups (Irish, African - American, Puerto Rican, Chicano, Dominican, Jamaican, and Central American). These gangs ranged in size from 34 members to 1000 + members. Members ranged in age from 10 - 42.

3.   See National Needs Assessment Research, Knox et.al, (1995).
      This research is based on a national survey of 1,994 self-reported gang members located at 24 different sites from the states of California, Illinois, Indiana, Iowa, North Carolina, Ohio, Texas, and Wisconsin.

REFERENCES

Blau, P. M. and Scott, R. 1962. *Formal organizations.* Chicago: Chandler Publishing Co.

Etzioni, A. 1964. *Modern organizations.* Englewood Cliff, NJ: Prentice Hall, Inc.

Jankowski, M. S. 1991. *Island in the street.* Berkeley: University of California Press.

Knox, G. W. 1994. *An introduction to gangs.* Bristol, IN: Wyndham Press.

Knox ,G. W. and Co-Principal Investigators. 1995. *Gang intervention and prevention.* Chicago: National Gang Crime Research Center.

Knox, G. W. and Co-Principal Investigators. 1997. *The facts about gang life in America today: A national study of over 4,000 gang members.* Chicago: National Gang Crime Research Center.

March, J. G. and Simon, H. 1967. *Organizations.* New York: John Wiley & Sons.

Olsen, M. E. 1968. *The process of social organization.* New York: Holt, Rinehard and Winston, Inc.

Padilla, F. M. 1992. *The gang as an American enterprise.* New Brunswick, NJ: Rutgers University Press.

Thompson, J. D. 1967. *Organizations in action.* New York: McGraw-Hill Book Company.

CHAPTER EIGHT

GANG ACTIVITY IN JUVENILE CORRECTIONAL FACILITIES: SECURITY, MANAGEMENT AND TREATMENT CHALLENGES

Sandra S. Stone, Ph.D.
State University of West Georgia

Alice P. Franklin Elder, Ph.D.
Ohio Youth Services

Youth gangs have been a topic of sociological inquiry since early in this century. Interest in youth gangs has heightened during the past decade, however, as juveniles have become increasingly involved in drug trafficking and violent crime. A substantial body of work has been published over the past few years documenting the formation, prevalence and activities of youth gangs. For the most part, these studies have focused on the street environment in which youth gangs flourish (e.g. Curry and Spergel, 1988; Fagan , 1989; Goldstein, 1991; Hagedorn, 1988; Huff, 1990; Klein and Maxson, 1989; Knox, 1991; Spergel, 1989; Vigil, 1988). In contrast, research on gang formation and gang activity in long-term juvenile correctional facilities is almost nonexistent.

A review of the literature prior to 1996 revealed no currently published studies that dealt specifically with juvenile corrections populations and few that addressed gang formation and activity in adult prison settings (Camp and Camp, 1985; Fong and Buentello, 1991). Fong and Buentello (1991) suggest that the lack of official information on "gang intelligence," security concerns and the "code of silence" of gang members are the primary reasons why research on gang formation in adult prisons is so rare.

Undoubtedly, the factors cited above are barriers to conducting research on gang formation and gang activity in long-term juvenile facilities as well. Additional barriers might also be the lack of awareness of gang activity in juvenile correctional facilities by facility staff, restricted access to juvenile offenders due to confidentiality statutes and the fact that they are minors, and political sensitivity on the part of facility and system administrators.

Increased gang activity inside secure juvenile correctional facilities has resulted in a heightened concern for safety and security among facility staff. In response to these concerns, some states have begun examining the extent and dynamics of gang activity inside their youth training schools. A study in Georgia (Stone and Wycoff, 1996) replicated a modified version of an earlier study that had been done in Texas in the adult facilities. Facility staff members were surveyed regarding their observations and perceptions of behaviors identified as being indicators of gang activity. Staff members were also asked about the degree of overcrowding, estimated percent of gang members in the youth population, whether they had received training in dealing with gangs, strategies used in the facility to address gang activity, staff assessment of gang formation within the facility, staff recommendations for intervention, and staff attitudes toward youths identified as gang members. Focusing on youths instead of staff, Franklin-Elder and Zheng (1996) conducted a survey of self-identified gang members in secure facilities operated by the Ohio Department of Youth Services. After documenting the existence of youth gangs in their facilities (approximately 46% of those surveyed reported gang membership), they discuss resulting security challenges, management concerns, and rehabilitation issues for states and private entities operating juvenile correctional facilities. The California Youth Authority has also studied gang activity in state operated facilities and has developed a Gang Violence Reduction Project in response (California Youth Authority, 1996).

In addition to these studies, the National Gang Crime Research Center conducted a major study of youth gang activity both inside and outside correctional facilities during the spring, summer and fall of 1996 – Project GANGFACT. The study included youths and adults from a variety of correctional programs in 17 states. The total sample size was in excess of 10,000, with approximately 4,000 self-reported gang members. The study involved the completion of a survey questionnaire that included questions about gang-related activities inside the correctional facilities. This work is, by far, the most extensive and comprehensive look at gang activity inside primarily juvenile correctional facilities ever conducted. This paper will discuss the findings from this large, national study and suggest additional research that can be done to further our understanding of the extent and dynamics of gang activity inside juvenile correctional facilities.

METHODOLOGY

The study was coordinated by the National Gang Crime Research Center in Chicago. Twenty-eight investigators in 17 different states administered a 99-item survey questionnaire to approximately 10,000 individuals, mostly youths, involved in a variety of correctional settings. The survey was anonymous and participation was voluntary. The completed surveys were then returned to the National Gang Crime Research Center in Chicago for data entry and analysis. A detailed report of the methodology can be found in Chapter Two of this book, or a full copy of the report can be obtained from the National Gang Crime Research Center.

The survey asked about many different aspects of the respondents' lives, including their previous and/or current involvement in gang activities. Only those questions relating to activities inside correctional facilities will be presented here.

RESULTS

The survey was administered to 10,166 individuals in different types of correctional facilities and programs in 17 different states. Of those, 4,140 or approximately 40%, reported having joined a gang. Of those who reported gang membership, 2,627, or 65%, indicated they were active members of their gang at the time of the survey.

Respondents were asked if they thought there was a connection between adult prison gangs and juvenile institutional gangs. A slight majority (54%) said they did think there was a connection, but what is more interesting is the difference between gang members and non-gang members. While some 44% of non-gang members thought there was a connection between adult prison gangs and juvenile institutional gangs, some 62% of gang members thought the connection existed. This difference between gang and non-gang members was statistically significant (Chi-square=187.6, p<.001).

For those respondents who reported gang membership, the survey asked if they had first joined a gang while in a correctional institution, and, if so, how old they were at the time. Some 28% indicated they first joined a gang in an institution when they were 12 - 13 years old; some 16% when they were 14 - 15 years old; some 9% when they were 16 - 17 years old; and 48% reported that they did not first join a gang in an institution. Further, some 61% of gang members reported that the gangs inside correctional institutions are basically the same gangs that exist on the streets.

The survey asked how many disciplinary reports the respondent had received while in the facility. There was a significant difference (Chi-square = 581.3, p < .001) in the responses between non-gang and gang members, with 56% of non-gang members reporting no disciplinary reports, and only 32% of gang members reporting no disciplinary reports.

The survey asked respondents if they had been in a physical fight with anyone while in the facility. Some 42% of all respondents reported that they had been involved in a physical fight, but there was a significant difference between gang and non-gang members (Chi-square = 639.6, p < .001), with

30% of non-gang members reporting being in a fight versus 57% of gang members.

Respondents were asked if they had started a fight or attacked someone while in the facility, and approximately 22% said they had. Again, the difference between gang and non-gang members was significant (Chi-square = 645.3, p < .001). While 12% of the non-gang members said they had started a fight or attacked someone, 35% of the gang members indicated they had engaged in this activity. Further, gang members were asked if they had fought with any rival gang members while in the facility, and some 40% reported in the affirmative.

The survey asked if the respondent had carried a homemade weapon while in the facility. About a fifth (19%) of the respondents reported that they had, in fact, carried a homemade weapon while incarcerated. The responses to this question were significantly different between gang and non-gang members (Chi-square = 345.6 p <.001), with 12% of non-gang members reporting that they had carried a weapon versus 28% of gang members.

The respondents were asked if they had threatened any facility staff member while incarcerated, and about a fifth (19%) said they had. Again, there were significant differences between gang and non-gang members (Chi-square = 470.3, p < .001), with 11% of non-gang members reporting having threatened staff compared to 30% of gang members.

The survey asked if the respondent had tried to smuggle any illegal drugs into the facility since being incarcerated. Approximately 15% did report trying to do so, and there was a significant difference between gang and non-gang members (Chi-square = 384.6, p < .001). While 8% of the non-gang members had tried to smuggle in illegal drugs, some 23% of gang members had tried to do so.

The survey asked if gangs used religion as a front in order to conduct their business in the facility. About 30% reported that gangs did, in fact, use religion as a front in order to conduct gang business. There was a very weak, but still significant, difference on this variable between gang and non-gang members (Chi-square = 7.06, p = .008), with 28% of non-gang members reporting in the affirmative, compared to 31% of gang members. In addition, gang members were asked if they had used "legal letters" to communicate with fellow gang members while they had been in the facility, and some 38% reported that they had, indeed, done so.

Another question on the survey asked if gangs sought to influence staff members to bring drugs and other contraband into the facility. Some 31% reported that gangs did seek to influence correctional staff to bring in contraband, and, again, there was a significant difference between gang and non-gang members (Chi-square = 30.4, p < .001). While 28% of the non-gang members indicated that gangs seek to adversely influence staff for the purpose of smuggling in contraband, some 34% of gang members reported that to be the case.

Respondents were asked if they thought a zero tolerance approach to gang activity within a correctional facility affects gang recruitment. The results here are not very encouraging, as 63% of the incarcerated respondents did not think a zero tolerance approach to gang activity would affect gang recruitment. There was a significant difference between gang and non-gang members on this variable (Chi-square = 58.9, p < .001), with some 42% of non-gang members thinking a zero tolerance approach would be effective compared to 33% of gang members who thought a zero tolerance approach would affect gang recruitment within correctional facilities.

As summarized in Table 1, the results from this survey indicate that, indeed, the presence of gang members in correctional facilities increases the likelihood of conflict and disruption and poses a threat to the safety and security of both other inmates and staff. The presence of gang members inside correctional facilities tends to alter the physical, social and emotional environments in those facilities, presenting special challenges to administrators.

Table 1

NATIONAL GANG CRIME RESEARCH CENTER
NATIONAL GANG SURVEY
GANG ACTIVITY IN CORRECTIONAL FACILITIES

ITEM	NON-GANG	GANG
CONNECTION BETWEEN ADULT PRISON GANGS AND JUVENILE PRISON GANGS	45%	64%
NO DISCIPLINARY REPORTS	56%	31%
BEEN IN A PHYSICAL FIGHT	30%	56%
STARTED A FIGHT/ATTACKED SOMEONE	12%	35%
CARRIED A HOMEMADE WEAPON	12%	29%
THREATENED STAFF	11%	31%
TRIED TO SMUGGLE DRUGS INTO FACILITY	8%	23%
GANGS USE RELIGION AS FRONT FOR MEETINGS TO CONDUCT GANG BUSINESS	28%	32%
GANGS INFLUENCE STAFF TO BRING CONTRABAND INTO FACILITY	28%	35%
ZERO TOLERANCE APPROACH TO GANGS AFFECTS GANG RECRUITMENT IN CORRECTIONAL FACILITIES	41%	33%

CONCLUSION

This study provides additional empirical support for the presence of gangs in correctional facilities and the negative impact those gangs have on institutional operations. Increasing numbers of gang members and increasing levels of gang activity in correctional facilities raise specific issues in regard to safety and security, management and treatment.

The initial challenge in terms of safety and security is a standard method for identifying gang members, gang groups and gang-related incidents. One way to address this dilemma would be for facilities and programs to incorporate the gang classification system recommended in Chapter Nine of this book. If that particular system is not adopted, then some other method needs to be put in place for assessing gang affiliation and level of overt gang participation as well as gang risk and threat. Other issues that need to be addressed in regard to safety and security include the following:

1) screening visitors;
2) surveillance and intelligence gathering;
3) segregating/non-segregating gang members from the general population;
4) levels of response corresponding to levels of overt gang participation;
5) distinguishing gang activities from routine, anti-social and delinquent inmate activities;
6) inmates' use of legal mail to communicate with other gang members; and
7) having rival gang members/groups confined in the same facility.

The presence of gang members and gang groups inside correctional facilities poses special challenges for managers and requires additional policies, procedures and training for staff. Managers need to institute a zero-tolerance gang policy for their institutions and assess their staffing needs to effectively deal with this element of the population. For example, managers may want to hire specialized staff who deal specifically with gang members/groups/problems and who coordinate the activities of an internal security threat group team. Specialized staff may also be helpful in the area of staff training and programming targeted for gang members. Internal intelligence gathering will need to become more intensive and more sophisticated. On the other hand, however, these increased interventions must be weighed against inmates' due process rights, and care must be taken to avoid unnecessary legal liability on the part of institutional staff.

Managers of correctional facilities and programs may also find it helpful, if not necessary, to improve their working relationships with other components of the criminal justice system and the larger community. A coordinated effort is increasingly required to reduce the threat of gangs both inside and outside correctional facilities.

Still a third area where gangs bring new challenges is that of programming. Especially for juveniles, it is important to institute anti-gang programs both inside correctional facilities as well as outside in the larger community. Programs may include teaching alternative conflict resolution skills, building self-esteem and/or a sense of self-efficacy, cognitive behavioral re-training, and entrepreneur/marketable job skills. Continuous evaluation needs to be conducted on these and other anti-gang programs to determine what is effective in reducing gang involvement both inside and outside correctional facilities. Further, services and programs need to be on-going as youths transition from correctional facilities back into the community, and effective supervision in the community will require increased levels of cooperation/coordination between law enforcement, courts, schools, corrections and the larger community.

In an effort to learn more about gang activity in juvenile correctional facilities, the following suggestions are put forth for future work:

If possible, obtain personal interviews with some of the incarcerated youths to get information on the formation of gangs and the extent of gang activity inside the facilities from another perspective;

If possible, review incident reports and other paperwork in the facilities to obtain additional documentation of the frequency of assaults, property damage, requests for protective custody and transfers, etc. to help substantiate the survey findings;

Provide training for staff at all levels who work in secure juvenile correctional facilities;

Continue to conduct research on gangs and gang activities to keep those who work in the criminal justice and related systems better informed;

Train and educate program managers, agency officials and other decision makers on how to effectively use research information to plan, design, and create effective gang control, prevention, intervention and legislative strategies;

Develop and implement a classification system that can assist staff in identifying gang members on admission to correctional facilities and programs; and

Continuously evaluate intervention strategies that have been implemented with street gangs and gangs in correctional facilities to determine if they are effective, and if not, how they can be modified to produce better results.

REFERENCES

California Youth Authority. 1996. *The gang violence reduction project: A non-traditional approach to combating the gang crisis facing America*. State of California, Department of the Youth Authority, Office of Prevention and Victims Services.

Camp, G. and Camp, C. G. 1985. *Prison gangs: Their extent, nature, and impact on prisons*. Washington, DC: U.S. Department of Justice.

Curry, G. D. and Spergel, I. A. 1988. Gang homicide, delinquency and community. *Criminology, 26(3)*, 381-405.

Fagan, J. 1989. The social organization of drug use and drug dealing among urban gangs. *Criminology, 27(4)*, 633-669.

Fong, R. S. and Buentello, S. 1991. The detection of prison gang development: An empirical assessment. *Federal Probation, March*, 66-69.

Franklin-Elder, A. P. and Zheng, H. 1996. *Survey research conducted with self-identified gang members*. Ohio Department of Youth Services, Office of Research.

Goldstein, A. P. 1991. *Delinquent gangs: A psychological perspective*. Champaign IL: Research Press.

Hagedorn, J. M. 1988. *People and folks: Gangs, crime and the underclass in a rustbelt city*. Chicago: Lake View.

Huff, C. R. (Ed.). 1990. *Gangs in America*. Newbury Park CA: Sage.

Klein, M. W. and Maxson, C. L. 1989. Street gang violence. In N. A. Weiner and M. E. Wolfgang (Eds.), *Violent crime, violent criminals*. Newbury Park CA: Sage.

Knox, G. W. 1991. *An introduction to gangs*. Berrien Springs, MI: Vande Vere Publishing Ltd.

Spergel, I. A. 1989. Youth gangs: Continuity and change. In N. Morris and M. Tonry (Eds.), *Crime and justice: An annual review of research (Vol. 12)*. Chicago: University of Chicago Press.

Stone, S. S. and Wycoff J. 1996. The extent and dynamics of gang activity in juvenile correctional facilities. *Journal of Gang Research, 4(1)*, pp. 1 - 8.

Vigil, J. D. 1988. *Barrio gangs: Street life and identity in Southern California*. Austin: University of Texas Press.

CHAPTER 9

A GANG CLASSIFICATION SYSTEM FOR CORRECTIONAL POPULATIONS

George W. Knox, Ph.D.
National Gang Crime Research Center

INTRODUCTION

In a recent issue of *American Jails*, the magazine of the American Jail Association, several researchers from a previous national gang research project of the National Gang Crime Research Center argued for the merits of a gang classification system in correctional institutions (Knox et al., 1996a). Behind bars a gang is also called a security threat group (STG) or a disruptive group or a security risk group. The idea is that if a classification system could reduce the injuries to other inmates and staff from the known risk of gang members, then this should be adopted as a policy and procedure inside juvenile and adult correctional institutions in the U.S. today.

In this chapter we provide Model 1 of the STG/gang classification system. This is not our final statement on the issue. This is a first salvo in an attack on the gang violence problem that plagues the American correctional system today.

THE IMPORTANCE OF STANDARDS AND POLICIES REGARDING CLASSIFICATION

Historically, only three organizations have spoken to the issue of standards for correctional management today: (1) the American Correctional Association (ACA), (2) the American Jail Association, and (3) the National Juvenile Detention Association. Of these, the ACA plays a more prominent role because of its power in certifying and accrediting most correctional institutions. The ACA has adopted numerous policies, procedures, guidelines, and standards on what to do and how correctional institutions in the U.S. should be managed and run. But the ACA has no standards, no guidelines, no recommended policies or procedures for the handling of gangs or security threat groups (STGs), just as the ACA has no such policies or procedures recommended for the abatement or prevention of racial conflict behind bars.

This might be construed as a classic case of "social lag," where policies lag behind the onset of a new problem brought on by social change, except for the fact that the ACA was a recipient of over half a million dollars for studying the gang problem behind bars.[1] So we must conclude that ongoing risks to the life and limb of inmates and correctional officers alike can be attributed to one thing: the fear of change itself.

Currently, there are some correctional facilities in the United States that do take gang membership into account in their inmate classification system. But nowhere will anyone find a policy operable in American correctional institutions today where the risks to staff and other inmates is systematically reduced by a valid classification system. One of the reasons for this is that such a system has not been developed, neither by the National Institute of Corrections nor by any other federal agency that may have responsibility for the development of this knowledge.

EXPLANATION OF THE MODEL 1 GANG/STG CLASSIFICATION SYSTEM

In the Model 1 gang/STG classification system, there are six different levels of classification for risk or threat. Each of these is explained below. Overall, in the total national sample we were missing data on only 7.9 percent of the variables used in these calculations, so the model was able to be effectively applied to the vast majority of the national sample.

Level 0 consists of anyone who has never joined a gang and who has no close friends and associates who are gang members. This is the basic "non-gang involved" offender. In Illinois today, the Illinois Department of Corrections, in response to an enormous public outcry about "gang control" in Illinois prisons, has now sought to convert one of its facilities to a "gang free" facility. To do this, the facility would need to include anyone classified as a level zero, plus anyone who had previously been in a gang but has truly "dropped their flag." Someone who had previously been in a gang but who has, for example, become an informant or defected from the gang, is technically not considered a level zero gang threat because of their extensive knowledge about gang operations (i.e., such a person would be a Level 3 explained below). The Level 0 classification included N = 3,330 of the respondents (38.6%).

Level 1 consists of those who have never joined a gang, but who may have between 1 to 4 close friends and associates who are in a gang. This is, in other words, a low level gang associate. This person maintains a tie to gang life, but it is not a strong association. The Level 1 classification included N = 794 respondents (9.2% of the confined sample).

Level 2 consists of those who have never joined a gang, but who have 5 or more close friends and associates who are gang members. This is a high-level gang associate. This person maintains strong ties to gang life, even as a non-gang member. The Level 2 classification included N = 939 respondents (10.9% of the confined sample).

Level 3 is a person who has at one time joined a gang, but who has quit the gang life. This is the basic inactive gang member. We do recognize that those who have cooperated with authorities in terms of helping prosecute members of the same gang deserve a lower threat rating. However, the current data is not amenable for adjustment regarding this factor. We recognize that someone who has cooperated with authorities is going to be a lower risk than someone who has simply claimed to have "walked away" from their gang. The Level 3 classification included N = 1,380 respondents (16.0% of the confined sample).

Level 4 is someone who has joined a gang, is still an active member, but who has never held any position of rank or leadership in the gang. This is the basic "active gang member soldier." This is the typical cannon fodder of the modern American gang. The Level 4 classification included N = 763 respondents (8.9% of the confined sample).

Level 5 is someone who has joined a gang, is still active in the gang, and who has held a position of rank or leadership in the gang. This is the basic "gang leader;" this level includes not only the top leaders, but also the middle management or henchmen, so-to-speak, of the modern American gang. The Level 5 classification included N = 1,415 respondents (16.4% of the confined sample).

THE MEANING OF THE RISK/THREAT VALUES ASSIGNMENT IN MODEL 1

The Model 1 gang/STG classification system is based on an additive index approach. It is, therefore, a scale that has a range of possible scores from an absolute low value of "zero" to an absolute high value of "five." There are six categories; thus it is easy to interpret the level of the gang threat/risk analysis made here.

(1) The lower the gang/STG threat rating level, the lower the risk of gang violence/disruption/threat inside correctional populations.

The higher the gang/STG threat rating level, the higher the risk of gang violence/disruption/threat inside correctional populations.

Model 1 is a system of classification based on known prior or current behavior of inmates. Further, it is one that this chapter will show appears to have some empirical support, if the policy interest is that of preventing and reducing the threat from gang members behind bars. Is it not arbitrary in the global sense because, theoretically, anyone at a level 5 can "work their way down" the scale of risk or threat. It is a fair system of classification because it relies entirely on behavior.

CAN MODEL 1 CONSISTENTLY DIFFERENTIATE DISCIPLINARY VIOLATIONS?

The first test we will subject Model 1 to is the simple question of whether it consistently and significantly differentiates the disciplinary code behavior of the confined population studied here. The variable we will be using is the question from the Project GANGFACT survey: "how many disciplinary reports have you had while in this facility?" This variable had a range between 0 to 5 or more. For the purposes of this test it is satisfactory to create a bivariate variable from this factor: (1) whether the inmate has had no disciplinary reports, and (2) whether the inmate has had one or more such disciplinary reports. This is, therefore, how the disciplinary report variable was re-coded for the purposes of testing Model 1 here.[2]

Our hypothesis, then, is that the lower the Model 1 gang/STG classification scale score, the lower the rate of disciplinary problems inside correctional institutions. Conversely, the higher the Model 1 gang/STG classification scale score, the higher the rate of disciplinary problems for these confined offenders. Further, to be a "consistent" classification system, the rates of disciplinary problems should vary in an increasing fashion up the scale of the classification system. Table 1 presents the evidence of this first test.

Table 1
Distribution (N) for
Whether Confined Offenders Report One or More Disciplinary
Reports While in Custody
By Their Respective Model 1 Classification Scale Scores

Had One or More Disciplinary Reports While in Custody?	Model 1 Gang/STG Scale Scores					
	0	1	2	3	4	5
NO	1642	254	253	419	208	330
YES	896	357	465	751	445	942
% Yes	35.3	58.4	64.7	64.1	68.1	74.0

Chi-square = 965.2, p < .001

What Table 1 shows is a steady upward progression of the probability of disciplinary problems at any level of the gang/STG scale. Further, the most remarkable difference in Table 1 is between the category of totally "non-gang associated inmate" and any level of gang involved or STG involved inmate! Only 35.3 percent of the Level zero inmates had disciplinary reports while in custody. Once we start up the ladder of the gang/STG risk or threat ladder, the numbers jump dramatically and continue to escalate consistently, until the problem "doubles" at the high end of the Model 1 classification system. We can conclude with strong evidence that, in fact, the recent efforts in Illinois to create a "gang free" correctional environment is truly a needed innovation in the management of modern American correctional institutions. Further, Table 1 provides evidence that the Model 1 gang/STG classification system does, in fact, significantly and consistently differentiate disciplinary problems among inmates in custody.

THE ISSUE OF INMATE SAFETY: COULD THE MODEL 1 GANG/STG CLASSIFICATION SYSTEM PREVENT SIGNIFICANT INMATE VIOLENCE?

It is well known in the field of corrections that people in custody, whether juvenile or adult, present the greatest risk to each other. That is inmates, not surprisingly, are prone to engage in fights. In the confined context everything takes on higher and greater meaning. A slight insult becomes, in the correctional environment, a symbolism of far greater importance than the act itself; sometimes inmates die as a result. Whether a gang/STG classification system can reduce this problem is the thrust of the analysis undertaken here.

First and foremost, correctional institutions are mandated under law to provide for the safety and well being of those confined. The issue raised here, therefore, gains increased importance as courts have had a tendency to aggressively micro-manage correctional systems along the same lines of concern. The intrusion of the judicial branch of government into the executive function of government (i.e., corrections) would appear unnecessary with regard to inmate safety if a gang/STG classification system could systematically reduce the threat or risk of violence to inmates from other inmates, in particular gang-involved inmates, whom it will be argued pose a greater security threat.

The statistical issue here is whether the Model 1 gang/STG classification system can consistently and significantly differentiate fighting behavior among inmates. The variable we will use here from the Project GANGFACT survey is this: "have you been in a physical fight with anyone while in this facility?" Table 2 presents the results of this test.

Table 2 shows the most "peaceful" correctional climate, defined here as a low rate of fighting between inmates, would be if those classified as Level Zero in the Model 1 classification system were kept physically separate from the other Levels. Only a fourth (24.8%) of the Level Zero group report being in a physical fight with other inmates. Similarly, one could assume with a high level of probability that fighting will occur among the Level 5 group, because the risk of fights more than doubles among the members of that group (63.2%).

Table 2
Distribution (N) for
Whether Confined Offenders Report Being in a Physical Fight
With Other Inmates While in Custody
By Their Respective Model 1 Classification Scale Scores

Have You Been In A Physical Fight With Anyone While In Custody?	Model 1 Gang/STG Scale Scores					
	0	1	2	3	4	5
NO	2117	421	434	632	297	485
YES	700	254	354	605	393	834
% Yes	24.8	37.6	44.9	48.9	56.9	63.2

Chi-square = 680.8, $p < .001$

As seen in Table 2, again, we find strong consistent evidence support-ive of the value of the Model 1 gang/STG classification system. As we go up the scale of the gang/STG classification system, we find a steady progression in the level of risk or threat of inmate fighting behavior. The issue seems abundantly clear: this health risk can be prevented by proper use of a gang/STG classification system. The wrongful death suits that family members file against correctional administrators could be significantly reduced if such a system were in place.

Some may question our intentions regarding the importance of re-ducing the threat of violence among inmates as a radical issue. We respond that we neither began this analysis nor have concluded this analysis with re-gard to any issue other than that of the primary topic of interest: the empiri-cal issue of whether a gang/STG classification system, if implemented, could result in the operation of a safer correctional facility.

Based on the results of Table 2, again we conclude with additional evidence that there appears to be strong support for the value of implement-ing a gang/STG classification system. Our data do permit estimation of the number of inmate-against-inmate assaults that could have been prevented if such a classification system had been in place. This particular analysis is beyond the scope of the present report, but may appear as a result of the individual initiative of scholarly work of the co-principal investigators that were involved in Project GANGFACT in a future work.

INMATE AGGRESSION: COULD THE MODEL 1 GANG/STG CLASSIFICATION SYSTEM HELP PREVENT INMATE ATTACKS ON OTHER INMATES?

That inmates provoke other inmates is an age-old lesson in the his-tory of correctional work. Some inmates are more predatory than others. Some inmates start fights just for the value of seeing what happens: will the offended victim "fight back?" If not, perhaps the aggressor inmate can ben-efit from ongoing exploitation of the victim. Sadly, but truly, some of these encounters escalate into violence levels far beyond the initial provocation. Inmates die routinely as a result of such inmate-versus-inmate aggressive attacks, involving the starting of fights or simply attacking another inmate.

The variable used from the Project GANGFACT survey is this: "did you start a fight or attack someone while in this facility?" We feel this effectively measures violent inmate aggression. The test for whether a gang/STG classification system, if implemented, could reduce this problem is provided in Table 3.

Table 3

Distribution (N) for Whether Confined Offenders Report Starting a Fight or Attacking Other Inmates While in Custody By Their Respective Model 1 Classification Scale Scores

Did you start a fight or attack someone while in custody?	Model 1 Gang/STG Scale Scores					
	0	1	2	3	4	5
NO	2560	563	602	908	453	753
YES	237	106	182	320	236	562
% Yes	8.4	15.8	23.2	26.0	34.2	42.7

Chi-square = 716.2, p < .001

Clearly, Table 3 shows again that the Model 1 gang/STG classification system significantly and consistently differentiates this behavior of inmate against inmate aggression. Those at Level 5 have five times the rate of aggressive attacks as those inmates in the Level 0 category!

We would like to draw attention to one compelling fact that emerges here, as illustrated in Table 3. With the rapid onset of the gang problem inside modern American correctional facilities, there may be a hidden blessing in disguise: the ability to identify risky behaviors among the inmates today may be much more clear cut and quantifiable than ever before. The hope, therefore, is that inmate aggression could be more effectively controlled given the implementation of a gang/STG classification system. If the bad news is that we see a steady upward progression in the risk of inmate violence the higher we go on the gang/STG classification system in Table 3, then the good news is that, theoretically, this violence could be significantly prevented given proper standards, policies, and procedures that took such factors as gang membership or STG "risk" or "threat" into account in the classification systems in American correctional institutions today.

COULD THE MODEL 1 GANG/STG CLASSIFICATION SYSTEM EFFECTIVELY IDENTIFY THE DIFFERENTIAL RISKS OF WHICH INMATES WOULD CARRY IMPROVISED WEAPONS WHILE IN CUSTODY?

Every security chief in every jail, every juvenile facility, and every prison thinks they know instinctively who is most capable of carrying an improvised weapon. The weapon of choice for most persons in the confined population is the "shank," or the homemade knife. Such weapons are deadly, often have the size and length of a sword, and can be fashioned out of metal parts from the most unsuspecting sources. A low level of technology is involved in the production of edged weapons behind bars; all one needs is a piece of metal, scraping it against the abundantly available concrete for sharpening, and to fashion a "handle" out of tape or cloth.

Currently in the United States, about half of all prison wardens (47.6%) report that prison gangs have resulted in an increase in improvised weapons production among inmates (Knox et al., 1996b). It is a major management issue for the safety of inmates and staff. The issue, though, is whether the Model 1 gang/STG classification system could significantly and consistently differentiate weapons carrying behavior among inmates. If so, then substantial public interest in the implementation of a gang/STG classification system would seem to exist.

The question from the Project GANGFACT survey that is used to test this issue is this: "have you carried a homemade weapon (knife, etc.) while in this facility?" The results of this test in relationship to the Model 1 gang/STG classification system are provided in Table 4.

Table 4
Distribution (N) for Whether Confined Offenders Report Carrying a
Homemade Weapon (Knife, etc) While In Custody
By Their Respective Model 1 Classification Scale Scores

Have you carried
a homemade weapon   Model 1 Gang/STG Scale Scores
(knife, etc,) while
in custody?

	0	1	2	3	4	5
NO	2551	560	636	959	513	831
YES	255	110	151	271	175	476
% Yes	9.0	16.4	19.1	22.0	25.4	36.4

Chi-square = 461.6, p < .001

In short, Table 4 seems to provide the strongest evidence yet that the Model 1 gang/STG classification system could reduce the threat of violence inside American correctional institutions today. Clearly, as seen in Table 4, there is a steady and increasing statistically significant function in weapons carrying behavior among inmates in relationship to the gang/STG classification system. Table 4 shows that the Level 5 inmate has four times the rate of risk associated with carrying a deadly weapon behind bars compared to the Level 0 group. Clearly, a conclusion that would appear to be supported by the research reported here is that violence can be prevented in the inmate population by the use of this kind of screening for risk classification system.

COULD THE MODEL 1 GANG/STG CLASSIFICATION SYSTEM EFFECTIVELY CLASSIFY INMATES WHO THREATEN CORRECTIONAL STAFF MEMBERS OR CORRECTIONAL OFFICERS?

By the latest estimate from prison gang research (Knox et al., 1996b) which surveyed adult state correctional administrators in all 50 states, some 37.2 percent of these facilities are now reporting that gang members have been a problem in terms of threats against staff. In about one out of five adult state correctional institutions (18.7%), gang members have also been a problem in terms of actual assaults on staff. Gang threats against staff are no longer a small matter affecting a minority of correctional facilities in the United States. In some states these threats have escalated into the assassination of correctional officers.

The Federal Bureau of Prisons now has its share of the national gang problem as well. As aggressive prosecution in the 1970s added significant numbers of gang members to state correctional systems, increasing their density in the inmate population, the federal prison system now has more than its fair share of gang members due to effective prosecution of gang members for violation of federal statutes.

Our test of the Model 1 gang/STG classification system for this factor is based on the Project GANGFACT survey question: "have you threatened any facility staff member or officer while in this facility?" Table 5 presents the results of this test.

Table 5
Distribution (N) for Whether Confined Offenders Report Having Threatened Any Staff Member or Officer While Incarcerated By Their Respective Model 1 Classification Scale Scores

Have you threatened any facility staff or officer while in custody?	Model 1 Gang/STG Scale Scores					
	0	1	2	3	4	5
NO	2596	563	620	931	498	790
YES	200	104	161	292	191	512
% Yes	7.1	15.5	20.6	23.8	27.7	39.3

Chi-square = 647.2, p < .001

Table 5 shows, again, the steady upward progression of the threat of violence to correctional staff and officers: the higher the gang risk/threat classification, the higher the likelihood of such a threat to staff or officers. Another way of interpreting Table 5 would be this: someone who must work as a staff person or as a correctional officer today has a 5.5 times higher likelihood of being threatened by Level 5 (39.3%) than by Level 0 inmates (7.1%).

CAN THE MODEL 1 GANG/STG CLASSIFICATION SYSTEM IDENTIFY THOSE INMATES WHO WOULD ATTEMPT TO SMUGGLE DRUGS INTO THE CORRECTIONAL FACILITY?

Here we put the Model 1 gang/STG classification system to one more test: can it effectively distinguish another common but major risk to the safety and security of a correctional facility --- those inmates who would attempt to smuggle in illegal drugs? This test is based on the project GANGFACT survey question: "have you tried to smuggle in any illegal drugs while in this facility?" Table 6 provides the results of this test.

Table 6
Distribution (N) for Whether Confined Offenders Report Having
Tried to Smuggle Illegal Drugs Into Correctional Facilities
By Their Respective Model 1 Classification Scale Scores

Have you tried to smuggle in any illegal drugs while in custody?	Model 1 Gang/STG Scale Scores					
	0	1	2	3	4	5
NO	2610	576	665	1030	522	916
YES	147	85	104	192	167	381
% Yes	5.3	12.8	13.5	15.7	24.2	29.3

Chi-square = 473.2, $p < .001$

Table 6 shows that only 5.3 percent of the inmates in the Level 0 group tried to smuggle in illegal drugs, compared to 29.3 percent among the Level 5 group. Table 6 shows, once again, that attempts by inmates to smuggle illegal drugs into the correctional facility are also a factor that is significantly and consistently differentiated by the Model 1 gang/STG classification system. The trend here, as in the other tests, remains true: the higher the threat/risk score, the greater the reported attempts at smuggling illegal drugs into the facility.

GANG FIGHTS BEHIND BARS: WOULD MODEL 1 MINIMIZE THE DAMAGE?

The survey included the question, "have you fought with any rival gang members while in this facility?" The question is applicable, therefore, only to Model 1 Levels 3, 4 and 5. Table 7 presents the results of this test.

Table 7
Distribution (N) for Whether Confined Offenders Report Having
Fought With Rival Gang Members While In Custody
By Their Respective Model 1 Classification Scale Scores

Have you fought with any rival gang members while in custody?	Model 1 Scale Scores		
	3	4	5
NO	909	419	678
YES	309	272	625
% Yes	25.3	39.3	47.9

Chi-square = 138.3, p < .001

As seen in Table 7, gang fighting behind bars is significantly differentiated by the Model 1 classification of gang risk. Gang fighting, on the streets or in custody, is usually very predictable: it is deadly in its consequence. Table 7 shows that at the low end of this scale, a fourth (25.3%) of those in Level 3 can be expected to fight with rival gang members in custody. However, this risk nearly doubles for those in the Level 5 group (47.9%).

COULD MODEL 1 PREVENT SECURITY BREACHES SUCH AS USING LEGAL MAIL TO COMMUNICATE WITH FELLOW GANG MEMBERS?

This is a modern scam arising from the onset of the rights of prisoners to have uncensored letter communications with their attorneys. The survey included the question, "have you ever used legal letters to communicate with fellow gang members?" Table 8 provides the result of this test.

Table 8
Distribution (N) for Whether Confined Offenders Report Having
Used Legal Letters to Communicate With Fellow Gang Members
By Their Respective Model 1 Classification Scale Scores

Have you used legal Letters to communicate With fellow gang members while in custody?	Model 1 Scale Scores		
	3	4	5
NO	900	419	639
YES	274	252	641
% Yes	23.3	37.5	50.0

Chi-square = 187.1, p < .001

Table 8 clearly shows that this type of security breach is also a factor significantly differentiated by the Model 1 gang classification system. Some 23.3 percent of the Level 3 group have engaged in this behavior, compared to half of those in Level 5.

SUMMARY AND CONCLUSION

No distinction has been made in the analysis reported in this chapter regarding sentenced offenders and persons awaiting trial, nor has any distinction been made between juvenile and adult offender inmates. We assert that the analysis conducted holds up regardless of these distinctions. Further, the more well defined the population, the greater the stability a classification system may have in terms of being able to prevent gang-related violence and disruption or threats to such a facility. The reason this is true is that all screening for risk applications must be "adjusted" or fine-tuned to a local population for best results. Regardless, we assert that even the Model 1 classification advanced here could be applied equally well with improved levels of safety for inmates and staff than are currently afforded by outdated systems of classification that predate the onset of the gang problem in the American offender population today.

This chapter has a clear message for correctional administrators. The message is this: the rising gang density among confined persons requires new management tools to effectively address a wide range of problems affecting the safety and security of the modern American correctional institution. The time may be right for a "gang free" type of correctional institution in all state correctional systems. It is not a "contamination" issue; it is, rather, an issue of simple risk management.

END NOTES:

1. The ACA received a grant from the National Institute of Corrections, along with an additional supplement, to carry out its version of an assessment of the gang problem in corrections. The report estimated that only 6 percent of the prison inmate population in the United States were gang members, and therefore empirically trivialized the threat of gang violence in correctional institutions.

2. For the record, the uncoded, or raw version of the same question ("How many disciplinary reports have you had while in this facility") produced an even stronger Chi-square value (Chi-square = 883.0) than that of the test case created here.

REFERENCES

Knox, G. W., McCurrie, T. F., Houston, J. G., Tromanhauser, E. D., and Laskey, J. A. 1996a. A security threat group analysis. *American Jails*, X(4), pp. 28 – 34.

Knox, G. W. and co-principal investigators of the 1995 Adult Corrections Study. 1996b. Preliminary results of the 1995 adult corrections survey. *Journal of Gang Research*, 3(2), pp. 27 – 57.

[1]endnote text
[2]footnote ref

CALL FOR PAPERS

The Journal of Gang Research

The *Journal of Gang Research* is a quarterly refereed journal and is the official publication of the National Gang Crime Research Center (NGCRC). The NGCRC is a not-for-profit organization founded in 1990 to carry out and sponsor large scale gang research, disseminate gang research information, and to provide training on gang issues.

About the Journal:
The *Journal of Gang Research,* during the last decade, has achieved a remarkable history of publishing empirical, policy, and theoretical pieces on gang issues. The journal deals with any topic relating to gangs, gang members, gang problems, or gang policy issues. The journal has a large domestic and international subscriber base.

The *Journal of Gang Research* is abstracted in the following publications: Psychological Abstracts, Sociological Abstracts, Criminal Justice Abstracts, and Social Service Abstracts; as well as in the American Psychological Associations's PsycINFO, PsycLIT, and ClinPSYC on-line databases.

Author Benefits:
In addition to receiving copies of the journal in which their article is published, authors receive a one-year free subscription to the journal, and are automatically eligible to be nominated for the NGCRC yearly Thrasher Awards giving recognition to exceptional contributions in the area of gang research.

Submission Information:
If you would like to submit a manuscript, then please send it in quadruplicate to: George W. Knox, Ph.D., Editor-in-Chief, Journal of Gang Research, NGCRC, P.O. Box 990, Peotone, IL 60468-0990.

Subscription Information:
The current yearly subscription rates are as follows: $85.00 if paid by personal check; $120.00 if paid by agency, company, or institutional check; $195.00 for all foreign subscriptions.

Journal of Gang Research

Subscription Order Form

Name:_____

Organization:_____

Address:_____

City,State,Zip:_____

Telephone:_____

    Domestic (U.S.A.) *Institutional* **Subscription Rates (U.S.C.)**:
HOW LONG OF A SUBSCRIPTION DO YOU WANT? (SELECT ONE OPTION)
  Check One:
__1 Year/$120 __2 Years/$200 ___3 Years/$300 __4 Years/$400
___5 Years/$500

    Domestic (U.S.A.) *Individual* **Subscription Rates (U.S.C.)** Check
One:
__1 Year/$85 ___2 Years/$160 ___3 Years/$240 ___4 Years/$320
___5 Years/$400

Definition of "Individual" and "Institutional" subscribers: if you pay with your own personal check or money order, then you are an "individual subscriber". All others (Government agencies, libraries, companies, law firms, etc) are "institutional subscribers".

Please enter my subscription to the *Journal of Gang Research*.
    Enclosed please find check or money order or government agency voucher/purchase order <u>made payable to</u> "**National Gang Crime Research Center**".

Return this form with payment or P.O. to:

          Journal of Gang Research
          National Gang Crime Research Center
          P.O. Box 990
          Peotone. IL 60468-0990

Why You Need to Buy This Book

This is the book that everyone refers to, but few have ever actually read, and few actually living today have ever seen the full unabridged version. This classic work in sociology has now been skillfully reprinted in its entirety. Most people living today, including scholars on gangs, have only read the abridged versions of this classic work on gangs. Now scholars and students can have access to the "data" that Thrasher provided in his 1927 original. This edition provides all 23 chapters; abridged editions included only 21 chapters. This book will be invaluable to students in the social sciences.

THE GANG:
A Study of 1,313 Gangs in Chicago
by
Frederic M. Thrasher

The full, original, intact version of the Thrasher classic: a book everyone makes reference too, but few have ever actually seen.

Published now under license from the University of Chicago Press, this important work in sociology and criminology is once again available in its full and intact form. Versions that were published in the 1960's were abridged editions, dropping chapters that few have ever read who live today. Also the "original gang map" that was only included in the 1927 edition, which perhaps only a handful of people living today have ever actually seen, is now once again made available in this 2000 edition.

ISBN 0-9665155-5-2
Library of Congress Catalog Card Number: 00-133629
Length: 250 pages, photo illustrated, softcover (8.5x11)

Price: $59.95 plus $5.40 shipping and handling

Order From:

New Chicago School Press, Inc
Post Office Box 929
Peotone. Illinois 60468-0929

Here is What People Are Saying About the book entitled
An Introduction to Gangs by George W. Knox.

LAW ENFORCEMENT:

"An Introduction to Gangs is a must for any law enforcement professional to provide a more in-depth understanding of the roots and current trends amongst street gangs in the midwest". Yale C. Pope, Gang Intervention Officer, Ottawa County Sheriff's Department, Holland, Michigan.

"The information provided in this book could not be duplicated by any other source. The details are excellent. Since I am from a rural area that has gangs north in Indianapolis and south in Bloomington I don't have the sources for information about gangs like those that come from this book. Mr. Knox should be commended for his hard work and details." Terry Weddle, Sheriff, Morgan County Sheriff's Department, Martinsville, Indiana.

"At no time in my five years as a Street Gang Investigator have I read a book that contains such an in-depth look into this subject. It provides knowledgeable research into the many questions investigators have when working with street gangs. This book is the best resource I have found on gang life and has certainly provided the information I can use in addressing our gang problems." Detective David L. Williams, Gwinnett County Police Department, Lawrenceville, Georgia.

"As a Georgia state certified law enforcement instructor, I have read and researched numerous gang related books, periodicals, and articles for gang information and intelligence for my gang training courses. Nowhere have I found such a detailed source of information on gangs as your book. It's like having several well researched and documented gang books all in one book. Complete with gang statistics, photographs, and survey results, this book is a wealth of information. From your chapter on the "Classification Factors for Gang Analysis" to the several "Gang Profiles" (which are some of the best profiles I've ever read) your book is a must for all law enforcement agencies. An Introduction to Gangs is one of the best sources of gang intelligence and information available today! Absolutely outstanding!" Walter J. Marchant, Jr., Gang Instructor, Georgia Public Safety Training Center, Forsyth, Georgia.

"Dr. Knox's latest edition of An Introduction to Gangs is a "must read" for any serious student or investigator of the growing gang problem in the United States. The book has one of the most well researched and well written summaries of gang theory that I have been privileged to read. This text brings together the history, theory, and current practices of modern urban street gangs into a single volume. I would recommend it for the book shelf of any library, researcher, student, or gang investigator. This book is a "definite keeper"." Lt. Gregg W. Etter, Sr., Sedgwick County Sheriff's Department, Wichita, Kansas.

"The book is a tremendous resource tool that is used daily. The contents and material contained within the covers is invaluable in the fight against gangs." Detective James K. Haskins, Rogers Police Department, Rogers, Arkansas.

"Working as a police officer and supervisor in a specialized gang unit, I find An Introduction to Gangs to be an accurate, up-to-date, and useful reference for street gang information. This book contains an enormous amount of historical data, research information, and internal intelligence on street gangs. The book covers the wide spectrum of street gangs, their structure, how they operate, and inside information from past and current members. Having this much information about gangs, in a single source, makes this book a "must have" reference on gangs!". Sgt. Michael Langston, Aurora Police Department, Aurora, IL.

"I found An Introduction to Gangs to be a very informative book, covering various aspects of gangs and gang life. It is very well written & a benefit to all who work gangs, ranging from the novice to expert". Investigator Richard J. Lutz, Lincoln Police Dept., Lincoln, Nebraska.

"An Introduction to Gangs is by far the most comprehensive and fact filled book that I have ever read. This book contains everything that a community needs to arm itself in their everyday struggle to combat street gangs. An Introduction to Gangs is a must for any law enforcement agency that deals with street gang activity. This book explains the history of each gang and how to diffuse or reduce the size of the gang with prevention and intervention techniques". Lt. Kevin R. Sproul, Dougherty County Sheriff's Office, Albany, Georgia.

PROSECUTORS:
"In order to effective prosecute gang crime, you have to first understand the mentality of the gang and of individual gang members. In order to thoroughly understand that mentality, you need to read this book."

"A rare treat: an excellent blend of theory and practical application that can be put to use by police officers, prosecutors, corrections officials and educators no matter what part of the country they come from."

"If you want to understand the gang mentality and the motivations of individual gang members (from the newest wannabe to the veteran hard-core leader), this is a must read." James G. Guagliardo, Assistant State's Attorney, Criminal Division, Kane County (Ill.) State's Attorney's Office.

ADULT CORRECTIONS GANG/STG OFFICIALS:
"The book An Introduction to Gangs is a warehouse of statistical, factual and background information relative to all gang/STGs based throughout the United States." Lt. Chuck D. Gobble, Illinois Department of Corrections, Dixon Correctional Center, Dixon, IL.

"A serious compilation of gang history and current information. I found the information very useful because of how well documented and accurate it is". Major Raymond Rivera, Conn. DOC, Litchfield, CT.

Why You Need This Book:
    Thousands of copies of earlier editions (1991, 1993, 1995, 1998) are widely available, but this new 5th edition includes MORE and updated information. Three new chapters are found only in the 5th edition: mass media, the impact of federal prosecution on gangs, and a comparison of organizational characteristics of gangs and cults.
    This is the single most comprehensive analysis of gangs that has ever been written. It was acknowledged by leaders in the field as being the first full textbook on gangs. It is widely used by those who work in the criminal justice system (police, prosecutors, corrections personnel, etc). A number of reviewers have concluded that this is the single most authoritative book about gangs ever written.

Newly Revised and Substantially Expanded

AN INTRODUCTION TO GANGS

5th Edition, 2000

by

George W. Knox

ISBN: 0-9665155-4-4
Library of Congress Catalog Card Number: 00-133631
Features:
    ••• 30 Chapters cover the gamut of gang issues (history, community, theory, law enforcement, corrections, prevention, etc).
    ••• A full-page photo or graphic relevant to gang life is included to accompany each of the 30 chapters.
    ••• Includes eleven useful appendices including gang profiles
    ••• Useful subject index and author index for easy reference.
    ••• Extensive bibliography
    ••• Discussion questions for every chapter.

Length: 720 pages.

Soft cover, 8 1/2" x 11".

Price: $59.95 plus $5.40 shipping and handling

Order From:

New Chicago School Press, Inc
Post Office Box 929
Peotone. Illinois 60468-0929

INDEX to Back Issues
for the
Journal of Gang Research

The *Journal of Gang Research* is the Official Publication of the National Gang Crime Research Center, Copyrighted by the NGCRC, Chicago, IL ISSN Number: 1079-3062

Note: Individal Back Issues of the Journal of Gang Research can be ordered directly from the National Gang Crime Research Center, P.O. Box 990, Peotone, IL 60468. Please check the Website for the National Gang Crime Research Center for price information. The Website for the National Gang Crime Research Center is: http://members.aol.com/gangdigest/journal.html

Research", by Key Sun.
"Joe: The Story of an Ex-Gang Member", by Jessie Collins.
"An Interview With Richard Cloward", by Jeffrey Paul Rush.

V1N4:
"Do Gang Prevention Strategies Actually Reduce Crime?", by Dennis Palumbo, Robert Eskay, and Michael Hallett.
"When the Crips Invaded San Francisco - Gang Migration", by Dan Waldorf.
"Fraud Masters: Studying an Illusory, Non-Violent Gang Specializing in Credit Card Crimes", by Jerome E. Jackson.
"Asian Gang Problems and Social Policy Solutions: A Discussion and Review", by Lee-jan Jan.
"The Legacy of Street Corner Society and Gang Research in the 1990s: An Interview with William F. Whyte", by Karen A. Joe.

V2N1:
"The Effects of Gangs on Student Performance and Delinquency in Public Schools", by Thomas A. Regulus.
"The American 'Juvenile Underclass' and the Cultural Colonisation of Young Australians Under Conditions of Modernity", by Judith Bessant.
"National Policy Neglect and Its Impact on Gang Suppression", by James G. Houston.
"Youth Gang Intervention and Prevention in Texas: Evaluating Community Mobilization Training", by Elizabeth H. McConnell.

V2N2:
"A Comparative Analysis of Prison Gang Members, Security Threat Group Inmates and General Population Prisoners in the Texas Department of Corrections", by Robert S. Fong and Ronald E. Vogel.
"The Gang Problem in Large and Small Cities: An Analysis of Police Perceptions in Nine States", by James F. Quinn, Peggy M. Tobolowsky, and William T. Downs.
"A Community-University Based Approach to Gang Intervention and Delinquency Prevention: Racine's Innovative Model for Small Cities", by Susan R. Takata and Charles Tyler.
"The Evolution of Gang Formation: Potentially Delinquent Activity and Gang Involvement", by Jeffery T. Walker, Judge Bill White, and E. Ashley White.
"A More Effective Strategy for Dealing With Inner City Street Corner Gangs", by Angelo Ralph Orlandella.
"An Interview with James F. Short, Jr.", by Eric L. Jensen.

V2N3:
"Gang Affiliation Among Asian-American High School Students: A Path Analysis of Social Development Model 1", by Zheng Wang.
"Predictors of Gang Violence: The Impact of Drugs and Guns on Police Perceptions in Nine States", by James F. Quinn and Bill Downs.
"Juvenile Gang Activity in Alabama", by Jerry C. Armor and Vincent Keith Jackson.
"Hispanic Perceptions of Youth Gangs: A Descriptive Exploration", by Marc Gertz, Laura Bedard, and Will Persons.
"Implications of the Shaw-McKay Studies and the Problems of Intervention in Gang Work", by Anthony Sorrentino.
"Findings on African-American Female Gang Members Using A Matched Pair Design", by George W. Knox.

V2N4:
"Female Gang Members: A Growing Issue for Policy Makers", by George T. Felkenes and Harold K. Becker.

"The Disaster Within Us: Urban Conflict and Street Gang Violence in Los Angeles", by John P. Sullivan and Martin E. Silverstein.

"Patterns of Gang Activity in a Border Community", by William B. Sanders and S. Fernando Rodriguez.

"Blood-in, Blood-out: The Rationale Behind Defecting From Prison Gangs", by Robert S. Fong, Ronald E. Vogel, and Salvador Buentello.

"Potential Research Areas for Addressing Gang Violence", by Shirley R. Holmes.

"Preliminary Results of the 1995 National Prosecutor's Survey", a report of the National Gang Crime Research Center.

V3N1:

"Gang Enforcement Problems and Strategies: National Survey Findings", by Claire M. Johnson, Barbara A. Webster, Edward F. Connors, and Diana J. Saenz.

"Delinquency in Chicago During the Roaring Twenties: Assembling Reality in Ethnography", by Karen A. Joe.

"Investigating Gang Structures", by Cheryl L. Maxson and Malcolm W. Klein.

"Victimization Patterns of Asian Gangs in the United States", by John Huey-Long Song and Lynn M. Hurysz.

"Tattoos and the New Urban Tribes", by Lt. Gregg W. Etter.

"Gang Profile: The Gangster Disciples", by George W. Knox and L.L. Fuller.

V3N2:

"Gang Migration: The Familial Gang Transplant Phenomenon", by John A. Laskey.

"Community Strategies to Neutralize Gang Proliferation", by James F. Anderson and Laronistine Dyson.

"Preliminary Results of the 1995 Adult Corrections Survey: A Special Report of the National Gang Crime Research Center".

"Gang Profile: The Black Gangsters, AKA 'New Breed'", by George W. Knox, Ph.D..

V3N3:

"What Works: The Search for Excellence in Gang Intervention Programs", by James G. Houston.

"A Violent Few: Gang Girls in the California Youth Authority", by Jill Leslie Rosenbaum.

"Specialization Patterns of Gang and Nongang Offending: A Latent Structure Analysis", by Kevin M. Thompson, David Brownfield, and Ann Marie Sorenson.

"The 'Tabula Rasa' Intervention Project for Delinquent Gang-Involved Females", by Ernest M. DeZolt, Linda M. Schmidt, and Donna C. Gilcher.

"Gang Profile: The Black Disciples", by George W. Knox, Ph.D.

V3N4:

"Inside Gang Society: How Gang Members Imitate Legitimate Social Forms", by Alice P. Franklin Elder, Ph.D.

"Defiance and Gang Identity: Quantitative Tests of Qualitative Hypotheses", by Gary F. Jensen.

"Factors Associated With Gang Involvement Among Incarcerated Youths", by William Evans and Alex Mason.

"Research Note: The 1996 National Law Enforcement Gang Analysis Survey".

"Gang Profile: The Black P. Stone Nation", by George W. Knox, Ph.D.

V4N1:

"The Extent and Dynamics of Gang Activity in Juvenile Correctional Facilities", by Sandra S. Stone, Ph.D. and Jerry Wycoff, Ph.D.

"A Comparative Analysis of Female Gang and Non-Gang Members in Chicago", by Jean Chang, Ph.D.

"Joining the Gang: A Look at Youth Gang Recruitment", by Thomas A. Rees, Jr.

"Common Characteristics of Gangs: Examining the Cultures of the New Urban Tribes", by Lt. Gregg W. Etter, Sr.

"The Rural Gang Problem: A Case Study in the Midwest", by Michael P. Coghlan.

"Research Note: A Comparison of Two Gangs - The Gangster Disciples and the Vice Lords", by George W. Knox, Ph.D.

"Special Report: White Racist Extremist Gang Members - A Behavioral Profile", by Thomas F. McCurrie.

"Gang Profile: A Nation of Gods - The Five Percent Nation of Islam", by G.V. Corbiscello.

V5N3:

"At-Risk Behavior and Group Fighting: A Latent Structure Analysis, by Kevin M. Thompson, David Brownfield, and Ann Marie Sorenson.

"Social and Psychological Characteristics of Gang Members", by Marc Le Blanc and Nadine Lanctot.

"Nickname Usuage by Gang Members", by Barbara H. Zaitzow.

"Prison Gangs in South Africa: A Comparative Analysis", by James G. Houston and Johan Prinsloo.

Special Report: An Update of Asian Gang Affiliation, by Zheng Wang, Ph.D.

Abstracts: The Preliminary Program of the 19998 Second International Gang Specialiast Training Conference.

V5N4:

"Development of an Instrument for Predicting At-Risk Potential for Adolescent Street Gang Membership", by Todd D. Negola, M.A.

"From Boozies to Bloods: Early Gangs in Los Angeles", by John C. Quicker and Akil Batani-Khalfani.

"The Death of Telemachus: Street Gangs and the Decline of Modern Rites of Passage", by Andrew V. Papachristos.

"Views from the Field: Guidelines for Operating an Effective Gang Unit", by Sgt. Michael Langston.

"Special Report: How to Gang Proof Your Child", by George W. Knox, Ph.D.

V6N1:

"A Special Report from the National Gang Crime Research Center: Excerpts from the Economics of Gang Life".

"Views from the Field of Law Enforcment: A Speech by Sgt. Ron Stallworth".

"Views from the Vield of Corrections: A Speech to Inmates by Major Raymond Rivera".

"Gang Profile: Association Neta", by Sgt. Raymond E. Hehnly.

V6N2:

"Risk Factors Associated with Gang Joining Among Youth", by Sandra S. Stone, Ph.D.

"The Promulgation of Gang-Banging Through the Mass Media", by George W. Knox, Ph.D.

"Views from the Field: Gang Homicide Investigatio", by Det. James Fanscali.

"Research Note: Asian Gangs", by Thomas F. McCurrie, Ph.D.

"Special Report: A Comparison of Gang Members and Non-Gang Members from Project GANGFACT", by the NGCRC.

V6N3:

"Goal Displacement at Leadership and Operational Levels of the Gang Organizatin", by Alice P. Franklin Elder, Ph.D.

"Skinheads: Manifestations of the Warrior Culture of the New Urban Tribes", by Lt. Gregg W. Etter Sr.

"Prison Gangs: The North Carolina Experience", by Barbara H. Zaitzow, Ph.D. and James G. Houston. Ph.D.

"Risk Behaviors for Sexually Transmitted Diseases Among Gangs in Dallas, Texas", by Bertis B. Little, Ph.D.; Jose Gonzalez, M.S.S.W., Laura Snell, M.P.H., and Christian Molidor, Ph.D.
Research Note: "Juvenile Gang Members: A Public Health Perspective", by George W. Knox, Ph.D. and Edward D. Tromanhauser, Ph.D.
Gang Profile: The Brotherwoods - The Rise and Fall of a White-Supremacist Gang Inside a Kansas Prison, by Roger H. Bonner.

V6N4:
"A Comparison of Cults and Gangs: Dimensions of Coercive Power and Malevolent Authority", by George W. Knox, Ph.D.
"Jamaican Posses and Transnational Crimes", by Janice Joseph, Ph.D.
"The Affirmation of Hanging Out: The U.S. Supreme Court Ruling on Gang Busting Laws and Their Consequences", by Lewis Yablonsky, Ph.D.
"Trying to Live Gang-Free in Cicero, Illinois", by George W. Knox and Curtis J. Robinson.
"Views from the Field: The Impact of Gangs on Private Security in the Workplace", by Melvyn May, Ph.D.

V7N1:
"Gang Prevention and Intervention in a Rural Town in California", by Karen Stum and Mayling Maria Chu.
"Gang Membership: Gang Formations and Gang Joining", by Steven R. Cureton, Ph.D.
"A New Breed of Warrior: The Emergence of American Indian Youth Gangs", by Julie A. Hailer and Cynthia Baroody Hart.
"Profiling the Satanic/Occult Dabblers in the Correctional Offender Population", by Curtis J. Robinson.
"Views from the Field: By Gordon McLean".

V7N2:
"The Impact of the Federal Prosecution of the Gangster Disciples", by George W. Knox.
"Views from the Field: A Look Into the Michigan Department of Corrections STG/Gang Program", by Robert Mulvaney, STG Coordinator.
"Legal Note: Additional Civil Suits Against Gangs in Illinois".
"Views From the Field: A.D., After the Disciples: The Neighborhood Impact of a Federal Prosecution", by Andrew V. Papachristos.

V7N3:
"A National Assessment of Gangs and Securty Threat Groups (STGs) in Adult Correctional Institutions: Results of the 1999 Adult Corrections Survey", by George W. Knox.
"The Preliminary Program for Gang College 2000: Confirmed Trainers and Presenters With Session Length and Abstracts/Bios".
"Information About Gang College 2000".

V7N4:
"Overcoming Problems Associated with Gang Research: A Standardized and Systemic Methodology", by Douglas L. Yearwood and Richard Hayes.
"The Gangbangers of East Los Angeles: Sociopsycho-analytic Considerations", by Gene N. Levine and Ferando Parra.
"A Corporation-based Gang Prevention Approach: Possible? Preliminary Report of a Corporate Survey", by John Z. Wang, Ph.D.
"Homicide in School: A Preliminary Discussion", by Shirley R. Holmes, Ph.D.
"Special Report of the NGCRC: Findings from Project GANGMILL".